COSMOS

IMAGES FROM HERE TO THE EDGE OF THE UNIVERSE

BY
MARY K. BAUMANN
WILL HOPKINS
LORALEE NOLLETTI
MICHAEL SOLURI

FOREWORD BY
STEPHEN HAWKING

ASTRONOMY CONSULTANT
RAY VILLARD

DUNCAN BAIRD PUBLISHERS

LONDON

Distributed in the USA and Canada by
Sterling Publishing Co., Inc.
387 Park Avenue South
New York, NY 10016-8810

This edition first published in the UK
and USA in 2007 by
Duncan Baird Publishers Ltd
Sixth Floor, Castle House
75–76 Wells Street
London W1T 3QH

Material from this book was originally
published in 2005 under the title
WHAT'S OUT THERE. This edition has
been substantially revised and
expanded.

This book is dedicated to Mark Levine
and to Andre, Patrick and Gabriel Soluri

Credits at Duncan Baird Publishers
Managing Editor:
    Christopher Westhorp
Managing Designer: Dan Sturges

Produced by Hopkins/Baumann
Designers: Will Hopkins and
    Mary K. Baumann
Picture Editor and Astronomer
    Liaison: Michael Soluri
Editor: Paula Glatzer
Managing Editor: Jennifer Dixon
Science Consultant: Ellis D. Miner,
    Ph.D.

Additional Text: Ira Mothner
    and Martha Fay
Index: Roberts Indexing Services
Color Management Consultant:
    Son Do, Rods and Cones
Icons: John Baxter

Library of Congress Cataloging-in-
Publication Data Available

10 9 8 7 6 5 4 3 2

ISBN-10: 1-84483-476-1
ISBN-13: 978-1-84483-476-1

Inquires regarding COSMOS contact:
<hopkinsbaumann.com>
or <solurispace.com>

Color reproduction by Colourscan,
    Malaysia
Printed in Thailand by Imago

For information about custom
editions, special sales, premium and
corporate purchases, please contact
Sterling Special Sales Department
at 800-805-5489 or
specialsales@sterlingpub.com.

Note: Any reference herein to the unit
of a billion indicates a thousand
million rather than a million million.

**ROSETTE NEBULA (NGC 2237)
IN THE CONSTELLATION
MONOCEROS**

GLOWING FROM THE ULTRAVIOLET
LIGHT OF YOUNG, HOT BLUE STARS,
THE NEBULA IS A PROMINENT STAR-
FORMING REGION. STRONG STELLAR
WINDS ARE CLEARING THE CENTER.

VISIBLE-LIGHT IMAGE
THROUGH 3 FILTERS
(REPRESENTATIVE COLOR)

NSF 0.9M TELESCOPE
AT KITT PEAK NATIONAL
OBSERVATORY, NOAO

3 MARCH 1999

1,500 LIGHT-YEARS
FROM EARTH

**THE ANTENNAE GALAXIES
(NGC 4038 AND 4039)**

THIS PAIR OF SPIRAL GALAXIES
STARTED TO INTERACT A FEW
HUNDRED MILLION YEARS AGO.
THE MERGER IS ONE OF THE
NEAREST AND YOUNGEST CASES
OF COLLIDING GALAXIES.

VISIBLE-LIGHT IMAGE

HUBBLE SPACE TELESCOPE
(EARTH-ORBITING)

21 JULY 2004,
16 FEBRUARY 2005

62 MILLION LIGHT-YEARS
FROM EARTH

FOREWORD
THE NEVER-ENDING QUEST

At the risk of incurring the fate of Prometheus, who stole fire from the ancient gods for human use, I believe we can, and should, try to explore and understand the universe. Our knowledge of the universe is constantly expanding, due in large part to our ever-improving technology.

In the last hundred years, we have made spectacular advances in our understanding, and probed deeper and deeper into space in order to further our knowledge. We have put men on the Moon, landed robots on Mars and sent probes out to the farthest reaches of our solar system. Voyager 1, for example, has been traveling for more than 27 years, and is now sending images back to us from approximately eight billion miles (13 billion km) away. This quest for information is key to our advancement, and the data these probes and satellites send us is not only informative, but deeply inspiring.

The images in this book represent some of the most up-to-date and high-definition data available. It is worth considering, that as spectacular as they are, they represent only the minute segment of the universe that man has been able to investigate. It is currently estimated that there may be up to 150 billion galaxies in the universe; the majority of these images are taken from just one – ours.

I do not believe we will ever reach the end of our quest for a complete understanding of the universe, and in a way, I'm glad. Science after finding all the answers would be like mountaineering after Everest. The human race needs an intellectual challenge. It would be boring to have nothing left to discover.

Stephen Hawking
Cambridge, England
Fall 2004

STEPHAN'S QUINTET

GALAXIES PULLED TOGETHER
BY GRAVITATIONAL FORCE

VISIBLE-LIGHT IMAGE

GEMINI OBSERVATORY NORTH
8M MIRROR TELESCOPE
WITH GMOS

12 AUGUST 2004

300 MILLION LIGHT-YEARS
FROM EARTH

START HERE

THIS IS THE VIEW FROM EARTH OF OUR HOME GALAXY, THE MILKY WAY

THE MILKY WAY GALAXY IS OUR celestial hometown. Think of it as a vast metropolis, with as many as 200 billion stars. But it is just one of a possible 150 billion galaxies in the universe. And it is where our solar family – Earth, the Sun and our seven sister planets – are found.

We're relative newcomers. Our solar system was formed no more than four-and-a-half billion years ago. There are stars much older than our Sun, most of them near the bulge at the center of the Milky Way. At the heart of this bulge is a black hole with the mass of three million Suns –

**A PANORAMIC
EDGE-ON VIEW OF
THE MILKY WAY
FROM EARTH**

INFRARED COMPOSITE IMAGE
2MASS
APRIL 1997–MARCH 2001
25,000 LIGHT-YEARS
TO THE GALACTIC CENTER

a region of such powerful gravitational pull that even light cannot escape from it. This central bulge of the galaxy is set within a thin disk of stars about 100,000 light-years wide (a light-year is 5.9 trillion miles/9.5 trillion km).

We and our Sun are located far from the center of the metropolis.

We're in a kind of suburb, out on a long arm of the spiral-shaped Milky Way Galaxy. The view is great. From our place in space, we can look both "in," toward the galaxy's center, and "out" – as far into space and time as modern telemetry can take us. Still, the vast number of stars we see with

the naked eye are all neighbors, fellow residents of the Milky Way.

Galaxies (after the Greek word "gala" for milk) come in many different sizes and several shapes. And all are made, not only of stars, but also of gas and dust and the invisible material astronomers call "dark

matter." We can't see dark matter, but as much as 90 percent of a galaxy's mass consists of it.

The Milky Way is not alone in our sector of the universe. It belongs to a small cluster of galaxies called the Local Group, which has some three dozen known members.

NEBU

LAS

WHERE
STARS
COME
AND GO

NEBULA

SPACE IS NOT EMPTY. IT IS FILLED with what we call "interstellar matter." This is a mix of gases — mostly hydrogen and helium — and dust, made up of elements such as carbon and silicon. This interstellar matter is the raw material of stars and galaxies. Interstellar matter can clump together to form clouds of gas and dust known as nebulas (from the Latin for cloud). A single nebula may contain enough matter to produce tens of thousands of stars.

We classify nebulas by how they appear to us. As the fashion statements of the universe, these objects can be dark and brooding or alive with color. Their behavior has many guises and is intricately linked with the life of stars.

The dense and compact clouds of dark nebulas, for example, are not clearly visible in the night sky. But we can make them out when they block starlight or the glowing gases behind them. Other nebulas are brightly lit. Reflection nebulas reflect the light cast by stars. Emission nebulas are lit from within by the radiation of gas molecules excited by stars inside the nebulas.

Nebulas are key players in the birth of stars. The incubation process begins with the contraction of dark globules within the nebula. Globules contract until they collapse under the force of their own gravity, precipitating the birth of stars.

Although emission nebulas are associated with star birth, other glowing nebulas are on hand when stars die. These are known as planetary nebulas or supernova remnants. They are formed by the gas and dust released by dying stars. Stars the size of our Sun will eventually form a planetary nebula. This means we can expect to see such a nebula in about five billion years, when the life span of our Sun comes to an end.

**A KALEIDOSCOPE
IN THE CONSTELLATION
SAGITTARIUS**

THE SNAKELIKE FIGURE
IN THE UPPER LEFT
IS A DARK NEBULA.
THE COLORFUL FORMS
ON THE RIGHT ARE
EMISSION NEBULAS.
THE RED DOT AT
CENTER LEFT IS A
SUPERNOVA REMNANT.

INFRARED
COMPOSITE IMAGE

SPITZER SPACE
TELESCOPE
(EARTH-TRAILING
SOLAR ORBIT)

5 OCTOBER 2004,
27 SEPTEMBER 2005

10,800 LIGHT-YEARS
FROM EARTH

ORION NEBULA COMPLEX

ORION IS ONE OF THE BEST-KNOWN constellations. It is large in the sky and easy to see. The red supergiant star Betelgeuse sits at the mythical warrior's right shoulder, the brilliant blue supergiant Rigel at his left foot, and three clearly defined stars, almost as bright, form his belt.

Clouds of gas and dust envelop the constellation, which is home to a rich array of nebulas, known as the Orion Nebula Complex. Producing tens of thousands of stars within the past ten million years, the complex is typical of regions throughout the galaxy that are prolific in stellar birth.

Close to Orion's belt is the most famous of all nebulas, the Horsehead Nebula (to the right of center). A dark nebula, the Horsehead rears up out of the gloom, silhouetted against the red glow of a large emission nebula. To the left of the Horsehead is Alnitak, the most southerly star in Orion's belt. Below Alnitak is the Flame Nebula, an emission nebula whose hidden stars cast a curious yellow glow.

Set in the hilt of Orion's sword is the Great Nebula of Orion itself (next page). Bright enough to be seen by the naked eye, it is an emission nebula lit by several huge, hot stars at its center. These are the Trapezium stars (the four brightest form a trapezoid). Near the nebula's core are also approximately one thousand young stars.

A COMMUNITY OF NEBULAS IN ORION'S BELT

VISIBLE-LIGHT COMPOSITE

ANGLO-AUSTRALIAN OBSERVATORY/ ROYAL OBSERVATORY EDINBURGH

OCTOBER 1979

1,400 LIGHT-YEARS FROM EARTH

**AN INSIDE VIEW OF M 42,
THE GREAT NEBULA OF
ORION** (LEFT)

AN EMISSION NEBULA
ILLUMINATED BY HOT
STARS AT ITS CORE. THERE
ARE MORE THAN 3,000
STARS IN THIS IMAGE.

VISIBLE-LIGHT IMAGE

HUBBLE SPACE TELESCOPE
(EARTH-ORBITING)

OCTOBER 2004–
APRIL 2005

1,500 LIGHT-YEARS
FROM EARTH

CONSTELLATION ORION
(LEFT)

STARS IN THE CONSTELLATION
ARE AWASH IN NEBULAS

VISIBLE-LIGHT IMAGE
BY BILL AND SALLY FLETCHER

PENTAX 6X7CM CAMERA
WITH 90MM LENS

24 OCTOBER 1998

1,600 LIGHT-YEARS
FROM EARTH

**HORSEHEAD NEBULA
(BARNARD 33)**

A GIGANTIC
DARK NEBULA
OBSCURES LIGHT
FROM EMISSION
NEBULA IC 434

VISIBLE-LIGHT IMAGE

CANADA-FRANCE-
HAWAII TELESCOPE

2001

1,500 LIGHT-YEARS
FROM EARTH

MOLECULAR CLOUD

VISIBLE SITES OF STAR BIRTH in our galaxy, the emission nebulas are strung along the glowing stellar lane of our Milky Way as seen from Earth. These nebulas resemble campfires in a forest viewed from far away. What can't be observed in visible light is the underlying "forest" that is made up of giant molecular clouds that store most of the star-forming mass of our galaxy.

Molecular clouds lie along the spiral arms of a galaxy where dust and gas pile up and compress along a density wave. They are so cold that primeval hydrogen atoms bond together in pairs. Hidden from the destructive blowtorch of radiation from stars, some areas embedded deep within a cloud are so cold they are near absolute zero (−460°F/−273°C). Most of the hydrogen gas buried inside a molecular cloud is laced with trace elements such as

WIDE-VIEW IMAGE OF THE EAGLE NEBULA (M 16)

RADIATION FROM NEWBORN STARS HAS CARVED OUT THIS AREA OF A GIANT MOLECULAR CLOUD

VISIBLE-LIGHT IMAGE THROUGH 3 FILTERS (REPRESENTATIVE COLOR)

NSF 0.9M TELESCOPE AT KITT PEAK NATIONAL OBSERVATORY, NOAO

15 JUNE 2000

6,500 LIGHT-YEARS FROM EARTH

oxygen and nitrogen, and with fine dust grains of carbon and silicon that are even smaller than smoke particles.

Giant molecular clouds can be hundreds of light-years across. They are 100,000 times denser than the atoms found in normal space between stars. Still, there are about one quadrillion more atoms inside a ping-pong ball than in an equivalent piece of a molecular cloud. Dark molecular clouds are turbulent, clumpy and chaotic. Light-year-wide globules buried deep inside these clouds fragment and condense, precipitating a flurry of star formation. About 10,000 solar-type stars are born inside each giant molecular cloud.

The torrential energy of newborn stars eats out gaseous caverns inside these clouds, like holes in Swiss cheese. Some burst out as brightly glowing "blisters" on the edges of molecular clouds. One of the best known of the glowing "blisters" is the Eagle Nebula.

CLOSE-UP OF THE "PILLARS OF CREATION" (LEFT) **EMERGING FROM A WALL OF MOLECULAR HYDROGEN IN THE EAGLE NEBULA** (PREVIOUS PAGE)

INSIDE THESE DENSE GASEOUS PILLARS KNOWN AS ELEPHANT TRUNKS, YOUNG STARS ARE FORMING

VISIBLE-LIGHT IMAGE

HUBBLE SPACE TELESCOPE (EARTH-ORBITING)

1 APRIL 1995

6,500 LIGHT-YEARS FROM EARTH

GLOBULE

WHEN NEBULAS PRODUCE NEW stars, the process starts with a lump within a huge, dark, cold cloud of hydrogen known as a globule. Some disturbance – perhaps an exploding supernova – sets things in motion. The globule contracts under the force of gravity. It becomes so dense and hot in the core that it triggers nuclear reactions which generate enough heat to stop the collapse – and a star is born.

Globules come in a number of shapes and sizes. There are huge globules, stretching for tens of light-years, and smaller globules that look like black bubbles when seen against a starry background or a glowing nebula. The globules at right, in a major star-forming region of the constellation Centaurus, were spotted by astronomer A.D. Thackeray in 1950. They stand out clearly against brightly lit gas and dust that has been heated by massive stars far hotter than our Sun.

Emerging from the walls of some nebulas are long, slender columns known as "elephant trunks." These phantasmagoric shapes, such as the Horsehead Nebula, are created when the blistering ultraviolet light from a nearby star boils away nebular gas. Dense globules can resist this photoevaporation, shielding the matter directly behind the globule. The globule and the dust-laced gas behind it form the elephant trunk.

THACKERAY'S GLOBULES
IN THE ACTIVE STAR-
FORMING REGION IC 2944

EACH GIANT GLOBULE IS
1.4 LIGHT-YEARS ACROSS

VISIBLE-LIGHT IMAGE

HUBBLE SPACE TELESCOPE
(EARTH-ORBITING)

FEBRUARY 1999

5,900 LIGHT-YEARS
FROM EARTH

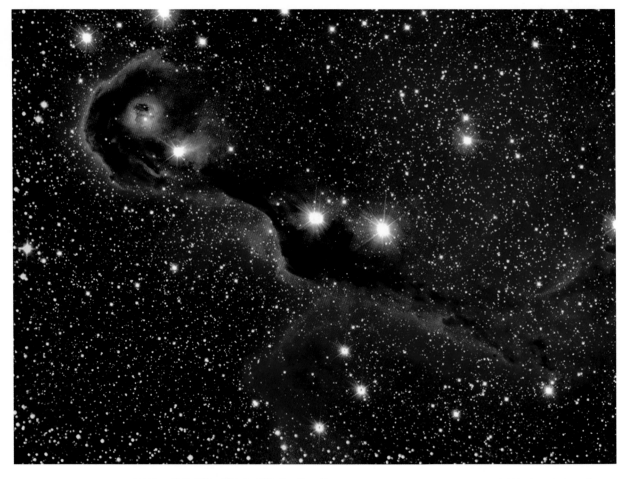

EMISSION NEBULA

THE BRIGHTEST NEBULAS ARE emission nebulas, which generate their own light. In fact, most nebulas we see in the sky are emission nebulas. These are clouds of hot gases, made up mostly of hydrogen. Light from emission nebulas comes from radiation given off by hydrogen atoms. The atoms have been energized by radiation from stars within the nebula or close to it. Most of the visible light seen from emission nebulas is called hydrogen-alpha (H-alpha), a special color of red light produced by warm hydrogen gas.

These stellar nurseries are where newborn stars and stars-in-the-making can be found. The images above show an elongated globule (called the Elephant's

Trunk Nebula) within an emission nebula in the constellation Cepheus, 2,450 light-years from Earth. The photograph on the left was taken in visible light. The image on the right was taken by an infrared camera. The infrared image reveals the formation of embryonic stars throughout the Elephant's Trunk Nebula. It also shows clearly the empty area at the head of the globule and the two young stars that have swept up the interstellar matter there.

Elongated globules similar in shape to the Elephant's Trunk Nebula can be seen emanating from the walls of many nebulas. These "elephant trunks" have resisted the photo-evaporating effects of nearby stars and are

ELEPHANT'S TRUNK NEBULA IN VISIBLE LIGHT (LEFT)

DARK GLOBULES SUCH AS THE ELEPHANT TRUNK ARE FEATURES OF LARGE EMISSION NEBULAS

CANADA-FRANCE-HAWAII TELESCOPE

2000

2,450 LIGHT-YEARS FROM EARTH

ELEPHANT'S TRUNK NEBULA IN INFRARED (RIGHT)

THE GLOBULE OF CONDENSED DUST AND GAS IS BUFFETED BY IONIZING RADIATION FROM A NEARBY STAR

SPITZER SPACE TELESCOPE (EARTH-TRAILING SOLAR ORBIT)

5 NOVEMBER 2003

composed of dense globules of gas and dust, as well as the shielded matter behind them.

On the following pages is the Flaming Star Nebula, with its illuminating bright blue star, AE Aurigae. Ejected from its birthplace in the neighboring constellation Orion, AE Aurigae zips through space at 220,000 miles (354,000km) per hour, lighting the Flaming Star Nebula as it passes through, which should take about 10,000 years. After that, the Flaming Star Nebula will no longer be appropriately named, for it will have lost its brilliant glow and will have faded to dark. AE Aurigae's intense radiation causes the nebula's gas to emit hydrogen-alpha light (shown in yellow) and to reflect light (shown in violet), making the Flaming Star both an emission and a reflection nebula.

CARINA NEBULA (NGC 3372)

HUGE STARS RIP APART THE MOLECULAR CLOUD OF DUST FROM WHICH THEY WERE BORN. COLOR INDICATES THE TEMPERATURE IN THE IONIZED GAS: BLUE IS HOTTER THAN RED. AT CENTER IS ETA CARINAE, ONE OF THE BRIGHTEST AND MOST MASSIVE KNOWN STARS.

VISIBLE-LIGHT IMAGE (NEAR TRUE COLOR)

0.6M CURTIS SCHMIDT TELESCOPE AT CERRO TOLOLO INTER-AMERICAN OBSERVATORY, NOAO

24–25 FEBRUARY 2000

7,500 LIGHT-YEARS FROM EARTH

**FLAMING STAR NEBULA
(IC 405)** (LEFT)

LIT BY AE AURIGAE (CENTER
RIGHT), A RUNAWAY BLUE
STAR FROM THE
CONSTELLATION ORION,
THE NEBULA IS BOTH AN
EMISSION NEBULA
(YELLOW) AND A
REFLECTION NEBULA
(VIOLET)

VISIBLE-LIGHT COMPOSITE
THROUGH 3 FILTERS
(REPRESENTATIVE COLOR)

NSF 0.9m TELESCOPE AT
KITT PEAK NATIONAL
OBSERVATORY, NOAO

21 DECEMBER 1999,
12 JANUARY 2001

1,600 LIGHT-YEARS
FROM EARTH

**MOUNTAINS OF CREATION
IN THE W5 REGION
OF THE CONSTELLATION
CASSIOPEIA**
(FOLLOWING PAGES)

THE RED COLOR REPRE-
SENTS ORGANIC MOLE-
CULES. THESE BUILDING
BLOCKS OF LIFE ARE
OFTEN FOUND IN STAR-
FORMING NEBULAS.

INFRARED COMPOSITE
(COLOR ADDED)

SPITZER SPACE
TELESCOPE
(EARTH-TRAILING
SOLAR ORBIT)

18 JANUARY 2004,
22 JANUARY 2005

50 LIGHT-YEARS
ACROSS

7,000 LIGHT-YEARS
FROM EARTH

NEAR AND MID-INFRARED

FAR INFRARED

**FOUR VIEWS OF THE
TRIFID NEBULA
(M 20) IN THE
CONSTELLATION
SAGITTARIUS**

**WHERE DARK LANES
OF DUST TRISECT THE
NEBULA IN VISIBLE
LIGHT, 30 EMBRYONIC
STARS CAN BE SEEN
IN INFRARED**

IN THE NEAR AND MID-
INFRARED IMAGE,
ASTRONOMERS CAN
COUNT THE INDIVIDUAL
EMBRYOS TUCKED
INSIDE DARK CORES OF
INCUBATION

THE FAR-INFRARED
IMAGE HIGHLIGHTS
COOLER CORE MATERIAL
FALLING ONTO THE
GROWING EMBRYOS

3 INFRARED IMAGES:
SPITZER SPACE TELESCOPE
(EARTH-TRAILING SOLAR ORBIT)
11 APRIL 2004

VISIBLE LIGHT: NOAO

5,500 LIGHT-YEARS FROM EARTH

COMPOSITE OF NEAR AND MID-INFRARED AND FAR INFRARED

VISIBLE LIGHT

**BUBBLE NEBULA
(NGC 7635) IN
THE DIRECTION OF
THE CONSTELLATION
CASSIOPEIA**

THE BRIGHT STAR NEAR
THE CENTER OF THE
NEBULA BLOWS A GIANT
BUBBLE OF CAST-OFF
MATERIAL. RADIATION
FROM THE STAR
IONIZES THE BUBBLE
SHELL, CAUSING IT TO
GLOW. MAGENTA WISPS
AT BOTTOM RIGHT ARE
REMNANTS FROM A
SUPERNOVA THAT
EXPLODED THOUSANDS
OF YEARS AGO.

VISIBLE-LIGHT IMAGE

NSF MAYALL 4m TELESCOPE
AT KITT PEAK NATIONAL
OBSERVATORY, NOAO

14 SEPTEMBER 2006

7,100 LIGHT-YEARS
FROM EARTH

**TARANTULA NEBULA
(30 DORADUS) IN THE LARGE
MAGELLANIC CLOUD** (LEFT)

THIS SPIDERY STELLAR
NURSERY IS GARGANTUAN
(1,000 LIGHT-YEARS ACROSS).
IF IT WERE AS CLOSE TO EARTH
AS THE GREAT NEBULA OF
ORION (1,500 LIGHT-YEARS
AWAY), IT WOULD FILL ONE-
QUARTER OF THE SKY.

VISIBLE-LIGHT MOSAIC
THROUGH 4 FILTERS

EUROPEAN SOUTHERN
OBSERVATORY
2.2M MPG/ESO TELESCOPE
AT LA SILLA, CHILE

27–29 JANUARY 2006

170,000 LIGHT-YEARS
FROM EARTH

PELICAN NEBULA (IC 5070)
(ABOVE)

LARGE DARK CLOUDS OF GAS
AND DUST ARE COMPRESSED
BY RADIATION AND STELLAR
WINDS FROM MASSIVE
YOUNG STARS (OUTSIDE
PICTURE AT LOWER LEFT),
CREATING NEW GENERA-
TIONS OF STARS. (THE
DOUGHNUT SHAPE IN THE
MIDDLE IS AN ARTIFACT.)

VISIBLE-LIGHT IMAGE

NSF MAYALL 4M TELESCOPE
AT KITT PEAK NATIONAL
OBSERVATORY, NOAO

28 OCTOBER 1997

1,800 LIGHT-YEARS
FROM EARTH

DARK NEBULA

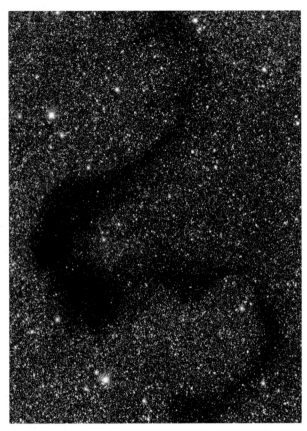

Dark nebulas and reflection nebulas are both gaseous clouds with no internal light source. We see dark nebulas by the absence of light — by the areas of darkness they create as they block light from whatever source lies beyond them. We see reflection nebulas in the starlight that bounces off their particles of dust.

The sinuous form on the left is the Snake Nebula, a chain of clouds that appears in a section of the constellation Ophiuchus. Interstellar dust grains — mostly of carbon — in this dense, dark nebula absorb visible starlight, leaving a snake-shaped stretch of apparent emptiness in the sky.

The emerging light show pictured at right shows the top of the dark Cone Nebula, a giant column seven light-years tall, in a busy star-forming sector of the constellation Monoceros. Radiation from hot young stars in the area has been slowly eroding the nebula for millions of years. The red halo that surrounds the column is caused by the glow of hydrogen gas as it is boiled away by the blistering ultraviolet stellar light.

**SNAKE NEBULA
(BARNARD 72)**
THIS LARGE COMPLEX
OF GAS AND DUST BLOCKS
THE LIGHT FROM STARS IN
THE BACKGROUND

VISIBLE-LIGHT IMAGE

CANADA-FRANCE-
HAWAII TELESCOPE

2000

500 LIGHT-YEARS FROM
EARTH

CONE NEBULA (NGC 2264)
PILLARS OF GAS AND DUST
ARE COMMON IN LARGE
STELLAR NURSERIES. THIS
CONICAL SHAPE IS PROBABLY
SCULPTED BY WIND FROM
A NEARBY STAR.

VISIBLE-LIGHT IMAGE

HUBBLE SPACE TELESCOPE
[EARTH-ORBITING]

2 APRIL 2002

2,500 LIGHT-YEARS FROM
EARTH

PLANETARY NEBULA

NEBULAS PLAY AS MUCH OF A ROLE in the death of stars as they do in their birth.

As a star ages and nuclear fusion changes from burning hydrogen to burning helium, the core shrinks and the outer layers expand. The star becomes a red giant, with a diameter that can be as much as a hundred times greater than before. Its gravitational pull weakens, and gas and dust peel away, forming a shell of interstellar matter around the exposed core. This gaseous shell is called a planetary nebula, although it has nothing at all to do with planets. It is simply that the astronomer who named them thought that the circular objects he saw resembled planets.

Planetary nebulas glow. In fact, generally they are not con- sidered planetary nebulas until

RING NEBULA (M 57) IN THE CONSTELLATION LYRA (LEFT)

A PLANETARY NEBULA OF GLOWING GAS ENCIRCLES A DYING STAR. THE FLOWERLIKE PETALS OF THE OUTER SHELL ARE NEWLY VISIBLE.

INFRARED IMAGE

SPITZER SPACE TELESCOPE (EARTH-TRAILING SOLAR ORBIT)

20 APRIL 2004

2,300 LIGHT-YEARS FROM EARTH

EGG NEBULA (CRL 2688) (FOLLOWING PAGES)

POLARIZING FILTERS REVEAL DUST SHELLS AND LIGHT BEAMS RADIATING FROM A HIDDEN STAR

VISIBLE-LIGHT IMAGE

HUBBLE SPACE TELESCOPE (EARTH-ORBITING)

SEPTEMBER–OCTOBER 2002

3,000 LIGHT-YEARS FROM EARTH

they start to glow. This happens as the dying star's core shrinks on its way to becoming a white dwarf. The gravitational contraction of the core generates heat, which emits ultraviolet radiation. When this radiation energizes gases in the shell of released matter, the gases fluoresce, emitting radiation of their own in a multicolored glow corresponding to different elements – green (nitrogen), red (hydrogen) and yellow (sulfur).

As seen on these pages, planetary nebulas appear in a variety of exotic forms, such as the flower-shaped Ring Nebula and the multicolored Egg. Some resemble animals, inviting descriptive nicknames such as the Bug Nebula, with its segmented form and winglike shapes, and the Cat's Eye, with its piercing one-eyed glare.

BUG NEBULA (NGC 6302)
(OPPOSITE)

THIS IS ONE OF THE BRIGHTEST KNOWN PLANETARY NEBULAS. THE FIERY, DYING STAR AT ITS CENTER IS COVERED BY A BLANKET OF ICY HAILSTONES.

VISIBLE-LIGHT IMAGE

HUBBLE SPACE TELESCOPE (EARTH-ORBITING)

AUGUST 2000

4,000 LIGHT-YEARS FROM EARTH

CAT'S EYE NEBULA (NGC 6543)
(FOLLOWING PAGES)

THE CONCENTRIC RINGS AROUND THE CAT'S EYE INDICATE THAT THE DYING STAR EJECTED ITS MASS IN A SERIES OF PULSES EVERY 1,500 YEARS. SUCH RINGS ARE THOUGHT TO BE COMMON IN PLANETARY NEBULAS.

VISIBLE-LIGHT IMAGE

HUBBLE SPACE TELESCOPE (EARTH-ORBITING)

4 MAY 2002

3,000 LIGHT-YEARS FROM EARTH

DUMBBELL NEBULA
(M 27) IN THE CONSTELLA-
TION VULPECULA (ABOVE)

ULTRAVIOLET RADIATION
FROM THE CENTRAL
DEATH STAR IONIZES THE
EXPANDING GAS CLOUD INTO
A COLORFUL DISPLAY

VISIBLE-LIGHT IMAGE

WIYN 3.5M TELESCOPE
AT KITT PEAK NATIONAL
OBSERVATORY, NOAO

19 SEPTEMBER 2002

850 LIGHT-YEARS
FROM EARTH

RED RECTANGLE NEBULA
(HD 44179) SURROUNDS
A DOOMED STAR (RIGHT)

THE LADDERLIKE
STRUCTURES
MAY BE CAUSED
BY MASS EJECTIONS
FROM THE STAR

VISIBLE-LIGHT IMAGE

HUBBLE SPACE TELESCOPE
(EARTH-ORBITING)

17–18 MARCH 1999

2,300 LIGHT-YEARS
FROM EARTH

SUPERNOVA REMNANT

THE BIGGER THE STAR, THE HARDER it falls. And blue supergiants — the biggest, brightest and hottest stars in the sky — fall hardest of all. When these stars have exhausted their hydrogen and burned away their helium, the core collapses until it releases a vast wave of energy, a supernova that blasts apart the remnants of the star and releases a mass of newly formed elements. The expanding shell of gas and dust that remains after this cataclysmic explosion is called a supernova remnant (SNR). It carries within it the heavy elements fused in the star's core and dispersed when the core blew apart.

The SNR begins a journey through the interstellar medium, transporting materials that will be used to spawn a new gen-eration of stars. All elements heavier than iron, including gold, are carried along by SNRs. Such elements are critical to the creation of rocky planets. Some evidence suggests that a shock wave from a supernova explosion four-and-a-half billion years ago triggered the forma-tion of our own solar system.

**SUPERNOVA REMNANT
CASSIOPEIA A** (OPPOSITE)

HOUSING A NEUTRON STAR, THIS REMNANT IS FROM A MASSIVE STAR THAT DIED IN A SUPERNOVA EXPLOSION 325 YEARS AGO — THE MOST RECENT SUPERNOVA IN THE MILKY WAY GALAXY

X-RAY, INFRARED AND VISIBLE-LIGHT COMPOSITE

X-RAY: CHANDRA X-RAY OBSERVATORY

INFRARED: SPITZER SPACE TELESCOPE

VISIBLE: HUBBLE SPACE TELESCOPE

NOVEMBER 2003–MAY 2005

10,000 LIGHT-YEARS FROM EARTH

VEIL NEBULA (NGC 6960)
(FOLLOWING PAGES)

THIS WISPY NEBULA IS THE SHATTERED REMAINS OF ONE OR POSSIBLY TWO SUPERNOVAS THAT EXPLODED 15,000 YEARS AGO

VISIBLE-LIGHT IMAGE THROUGH 3 FILTERS (REPRESENTATIVE COLOR)

NSF 0.9M TELESCOPE AT KITT PEAK NATIONAL OBSERVATORY, NOAO

14 SEPTEMBER 2000

1,400 LIGHT-YEARS FROM EARTH

REFLECTION NEBULA

WHILE EMISSION NEBULAS generate their own light, reflection nebulas are dependent on the illumination of stars. These nebulas are visible from Earth only when there is light from nearby stars for them to reflect. In an effect known as scattering, the bright light of the star is deflected off the dust of the nebula. Reflection nebulas are usually blue, because blue light is more readily deflected than red.

Illuminated by bright stars like scribbles in the sky, the blue nebulas here are located in the Chamaeleon constellation. Reflection nebulas, like emission nebulas, are often the site of star birth. In the thick dust of

the dark molecular clouds at lower right, new stars are being born. At 450 light-years from Earth, this complex is one of the closest star hatcheries.

Another is the Witch Head Nebula on the following pages. Peering into this dusty nest with infrared light, a telescope reveals embryonic stars nestled in their natal gas cloud.

The fragility of nebulas can be seen near the star Merope (page 63). Radiation from the star, one of the brightest in the Pleiades cluster, illuminates a reflection nebula even while destroying it. As the star cluster drifts through the nebula, the nebula is being torn apart by Merope's blistering radiation.

REFLECTION NEBULAS IN THE CONSTELLATION CHAMAELEON

THE COLORFUL NEBULAS CONTAIN SMALL DUST PARTICLES THAT REFLECT THE LIGHT OF THE STARS THAT ILLUMINATE THEM. THE BRIGHT STAR AT THE CENTER HAS TWICE THE MASS OF OUR SUN.

VISIBLE-LIGHT IMAGE

EUROPEAN SOUTHERN OBSERVATORY
8.2M VLT ANTU

JANUARY 1999

450 LIGHT-YEARS FROM EARTH

**WITCH HEAD NEBULA
(IC 2118) IN THE
CONSTELLATION ORION**

THE WISPS OF GREEN
ARE CARBON-RICH
MOLECULES, WHICH ARE
FOUND ON BARBECUE
GRILLS AND IN CAR
EXHAUST FUMES ON
EARTH. THE PINK DOTS
ARE INFANT STARS.

INFRARED IMAGE

SPITZER SPACE
TELESCOPE
(EARTH-TRAILING
SOLAR ORBIT)

10 MARCH 2005,
24, 30 MARCH 2006

800 LIGHT-YEARS
FROM EARTH

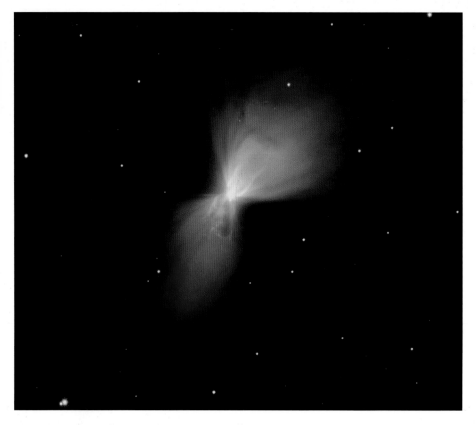

BOOMERANG NEBULA, ONE OF THE COLDEST PLACES KNOWN IN THE UNIVERSE (ABOVE)

IN AN EJECTION PROCESS KNOWN AS BIPOLAR OUT-FLOW, A CENTRAL RED GIANT CREATES TWO SYMMETRICAL LOBES OF GAS AND DUST. THIS BOW TIE SHINES WITH THE REFLECTED LIGHT OF THE STAR.

VISIBLE-LIGHT IMAGE

HUBBLE SPACE TELESCOPE (EARTH-ORBITING)

JANUARY–MAY 2005

5,000 LIGHT-YEARS FROM EARTH

BARNARD'S MEROPE NEBULA (IC 349) IN THE PLEIADES STAR CLUSTER (OPPOSITE)

A REFLECTION NEBULA LIT BY RADIATION FROM THE STAR MEROPE (OUTSIDE THE IMAGE, UPPER RIGHT)

VISIBLE-LIGHT IMAGE

HUBBLE SPACE TELESCOPE (EARTH-ORBITING)

19 SEPTEMBER 1999

380 LIGHT-YEARS FROM EARTH

NGC 1333 EXEMPLIFIES THE CHAOS OF STAR BIRTH (FOLLOWING PAGES)

THE PHANTOM SHAPES IN YELLOW AND GREEN ARE IN THE DENSEST PART OF THE NEBULA. THEY ARE GLOWING SHOCK FRONTS GENERATED BY MATERIAL SPOUTING FROM EMBRYONIC STARS AS IT PLOWS INTO COLD, THICK GAS.

INFRARED IMAGE

SPITZER SPACE TELESCOPE (EARTH-TRAILING SOLAR ORBIT)

10 FEBRUARY, 8 SEPTEMBER 2004

1,000 LIGHT-YEARS FROM EARTH

STA

ARS

HIGH
ON
ENERGY

STAR

Humanity has always been fascinated by stars. In antiquity, people thought they were holes in the roof of the world. Through them, they believed, one could see fires burning outside. To the ancient Greeks, anything in the sky, other than the Sun and the Moon, was called a star. Planets were "wandering stars" and comets "stars with hair."

Stars, of course, are suns – like our Sun – balls of gas that generate energy and emit radiation. They come in a wide range of sizes, but all lie within an upper and lower weight limit on the stellar scale. Red dwarf stars, for example, can have less than one-tenth the mass of our Sun. That's about as lightweight as a star can be for nuclear fusion to occur in its core and starshine to come about. Most stars in our galaxy are red dwarfs.

Blue supergiants are the heavyweights, at the upper end of the scale. Scientists suspect that blue supergiants actually have a weight limit no more than 150 times the mass of our Sun.

For a star, its mass – the amount of matter it contains – determines its destiny. The greater the mass, the hotter and brighter it burns. And temperature dictates color. The hottest stars (above 45,000°F/

25,000°C) are blue. Blue supergiants are even hotter because they burn hydrogen at a faster rate. The coolest stars (below 6,000°F/3,200°C) are red. Others are yellow, like our Sun. Mass also determines the length of a star's life cycle. The more massive the star, the faster it burns and the more quickly it consumes itself. So stars that keep cool live longer by burning slower.

An infant star begins life in the cold and dark. Birthing occurs within globules, dense clouds of hydrogen found in nebulas. Under the force of gravity, the globule shrinks and collapses, creating what are known as protostars. The protostar continues to contract until the heat and pressure are intense enough to set off nuclear fusion. It is now a star.

The protostar stage is only a small fraction of the total life of the star. Once mature, stars remain stable for most of their lives. Nuclear fusion – converting hydrogen to helium in the star's hot core – releases vast amounts of energy. But, eventually, the core's hydrogen is depleted. Nuclear fusion subsides. The core contracts and the star enlarges, burning the hydrogen in its outer atmosphere. It becomes a red

FIRESTORM NEBULA (NGC 604)

THE LARGEST KNOWN CAULDRON OF STAR BIRTH

VISIBLE-LIGHT IMAGE

HUBBLE SPACE TELESCOPE (EARTH-ORBITING)

JULY 1994, JANUARY 1995, DECEMBER 2001

2.7 MILLION LIGHT-YEARS FROM EARTH

giant. Nuclear fusion resumes and changes from burning hydrogen to burning helium.

What happens when all the helium is consumed is again a question of mass. Massive stars collapse in on themselves, lighting up the sky in gigantic explosions called supernovas.

The fate of the core also depends on mass. Stars with the most massive cores implode to form black holes, regions of immense gravitational pull. Less massive cores become neutron stars, with a diameter of only about 12 miles (19km) but of unimaginable density.

Modest stars like our medium-size Sun never get hot enough for such a flashy end. The gas and dust are released to form a planetary nebula that eventually disperses. The core contracts to a white dwarf — a small, dense star about the size of Earth with a mass like the Sun's. In time, when its remaining energy is spent, it literally fades away.

**A STELLAR NURSERY
IN THE DR 21 REGION OF THE
CONSTELLATION CYGNUS**

INFRARED LIGHT SEES
INSIDE A SHROUD OF
DUST TO CAPTURE MASSIVE
STARS BEING BORN

COMPOSITE OF INFRARED
AND VISIBLE-LIGHT IMAGES

SPITZER SPACE TELESCOPE
(EARTH-TRAILING SOLAR ORBIT)

11 OCTOBER,
22 NOVEMBER 2003

6,200 LIGHT-YEARS FROM EARTH

PROTOSTAR

Stars are formed when dense clouds of interstellar matter contract and fragment into increasingly small clumps of matter. Under the force of gravity, the center of a clump forms what is known as a protostar. As the protostar rotates, the remains of the collapsing dust cloud swirl around it, forming a disk.

The protostar grows as material from the disk is drawn or "falls" into it. When large chunks of this material strike the protostar, they release blasts of dense gas called "jets." The jets become visible as they blast their way through the opaque clouds of matter surrounding the embryonic star. And it is the jets seen here that reveal the presence of the otherwise invisible protostar.

Herbig-Haro (HH) objects are unusual emission nebulas that take shape as the protostar's gas jets collide at high speed with nearby material of the parent nebula. They are transient clouds that dissipate as the protostar approaches full stardom.

Protostars generate energy by compressing their gases. As they grow denser and attract more matter, gravitational pull strengthens, the motion of matter increases, and the temperature rises. Nuclear fusion begins when the protostar's core heats up sufficiently for hydrogen to fuse into helium. At this point the protostar becomes a young star.

THE PROTOSTAR HH 46/47 EJECTS SUPERSONIC GAS JETS IN A BIPOLAR OUTFLOW (LEFT)

THIS OUTFLOW IS ASSOCIATED WITH THE PRESENCE OF CIR-CUMSTELLAR DISKS THAT SURROUND YOUNG STARS. FROM SUCH DISKS PLANETS ARE BORN.

INFRARED IMAGE

SPITZER SPACE TELESCOPE (EARTH-TRAILING SOLAR ORBIT)

19 NOVEMBER 2003

1,140 LIGHT-YEARS FROM EARTH

THE TORNADOLIKE FEATURE OF THE PROTOSTAR HH 49/50 IS CAUSED BY A SHOCK FRONT FROM THE JET OF THE YOUNG STAR (ABOVE)

THE JET OF GAS FROM THE PROTOSTAR (OFF UPPER EDGE) IS MOVING DOWNWARD AT MORE THAN 100 MILES (160KM) PER SECOND, CAUSING SURROUNDING DUST TO HEAT AND GLOW.

INFRARED IMAGE

SPITZER SPACE TELESCOPE (EARTH-TRAILING SOLAR ORBIT)

19 FEBRUARY–2 SEPTEMBER 2004

450 LIGHT-YEARS FROM EARTH

STAR CLUSTER

THE PLEIADES OPEN STAR CLUSTER IN THE CONSTELLATION TAURUS

VISIBLE-LIGHT COMPOSITE THROUGH RED, GREEN AND BLUE FILTERS

SAMUEL OSCHIN 48-INCH SCHMIDT TELESCOPE AT PALOMAR OBSERVATORY

5 NOVEMBER 1986–
11 SEPTEMBER 1996

440 LIGHT-YEARS FROM EARTH

CELESTIAL BODIES ARE A companionable lot. They hang out together, and they tend to hang out with their own kind. Stars, for example, come in clusters, and there are two types. Young stars are most likely to be found in the smaller, more loosely structured "open" clusters, while older stars generally make up the more highly structured "globular" clusters.

The young stars in an open cluster were all formed at approximately the same time within the same cloud of dust and gas. Because of their youth, these stars burn hot and bright. The clusters they form are loose and uncrowded. This is because of the weakness of their gravitational fields, which are often too frail to keep them together.

Open clusters tend to be found along the arms of spiral galaxies, where there is new star formation. There are many open clusters in our own Milky Way. Among them are the stars of the Pleiades (right) in the constellation Taurus — the easiest cluster to spot with the naked eye.

Globular clusters, by contrast, are huge. They contain a tightly knit throng of stars — from 100,000 to one million — and are usually spherical in shape. Among the oldest structures in

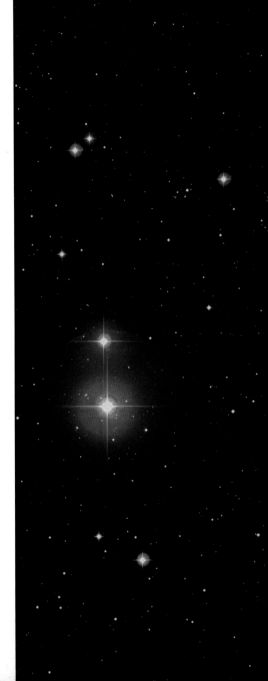

the universe, globular clusters were the first inhabitants of our galaxy. They are generally found outside the galaxy's disk, far from the star-forming regions. They are not involved in the galaxy's general rotation. Instead, they follow orbits of their own around the galactic center. In the Milky Way, about 150 globular clusters travel above and below the galactic plane in the halo, the spherical area that envelops the galaxy.

Globular clusters hold some of the oldest stars in our galaxy. The biggest and brightest of these clusters is Omega Centauri, with stars 12 billion years old. Some 17,000 light-years away, it resembles a small cloud in the southern sky. It, too, can be seen with the naked eye.

Omega Centauri contains several million stars, so densely packed that they occasionally collide. When they do, it is believed that they merge to create hot blue stars.

GLOBULAR CLUSTER 47 TUCANAE
NICKNAMED 47 TUC, ONLY OMEGA CENTAURI SURPASSES IT IN SIZE AND BRIGHTNESS. THE MAIN IMAGE IS AN ENLARGEMENT OF THE CONGESTED CENTER OF THE IMAGE ABOVE.

BY TRACKING THE STARS' VELOCITIES, HUBBLE DETERMINED THAT HEAVIER STARS SLOW DOWN AND SINK TO THE CLUSTER'S CORE, WHILE LIGHTER STARS SPEED UP AND TRAVEL TO THE PERIPHERY

VISIBLE-LIGHT IMAGES

ABOVE: EUROPEAN SOUTHERN OBSERVATORY, VLT KUEYEN, UT2 + FORS 1, 2001

RIGHT: HUBBLE SPACE TELESCOPE (EARTH-ORBITING) OCTOBER 1995—JULY 2002

15,000 LIGHT-YEARS FROM EARTH

BROWN DWARF

**BROWN DWARFS SURROUND
THE MASSIVE CENTRAL STARS OF
THE TRAPEZIUM CLUSTER
IN THE GREAT NEBULA OF ORION**

BROWN DWARFS, TOO DIM
TO BE SEEN IN VISIBLE
LIGHT (RIGHT),
POP OUT IN INFRARED
(PAGE 81)

RIGHT: VISIBLE-LIGHT MOSAIC
(COLOR ADDED)
PAGE 81: NEAR-INFRARED IMAGE

HUBBLE SPACE TELESCOPE
(EARTH-ORBITING)

RIGHT: 1994–1995
PAGE 81: 17 JANUARY 1998

1,500 LIGHT-YEARS FROM EARTH

Brown dwarfs are what astronomers call "failed stars." They have about the same diameter as Jupiter but at least ten times the mass. However, their mass is still too low to produce the high temperatures necessary for nuclear fusion. Cool and dim, with a surface temperature below 4,500 °F (2,500 °C), brown dwarfs are a hundred thousand to a million times fainter than our Sun, at least for most of their lives. For a brief period while young they are relatively bright, yet they are still a hundred to a thousand times less luminous than our central star.

The faint light may explain why no brown dwarfs were discovered before 1995. Since then, telescopes with sensitive infrared detectors have located several hundred. In a celestial population that includes both stars and brown dwarfs, if there are a hundred billion stars in our galaxy there are about five to ten billion brown dwarfs.

The same process that forms normal stars also forms brown dwarfs. But in their case, there is just not enough gas

available to reach true stellar mass and they are unable to fuse hydrogen. Early in life, however, brown dwarfs are capable of generating energy by burning deuterium (heavy hydrogen). But when this gas is exhausted after several tens of millions of years, the release of gravitational energy allows brown dwarfs to continue to glow as they slowly contract.

In 2004, a planet-forming disk was spotted by the Spitzer Space Telescope around a brown dwarf only 15 times the mass of Jupiter. The brown dwarf, known as OTS 44, is an extremely low-mass version near the dividing line between planets and stars. "It's fascinating to think that there could be miniature solar systems out there in which planets orbit objects that themselves are almost as small as planets," said Dr Kevin Luhman of the Harvard-Smithsonian Center for Astrophysics and lead investigator of the study.

Planet-forming disks provide the construction materials for planets to coalesce. The dusty disk surrounding OTS 44 has enough mass to build a small gas giant planet and a few rocky ones. Could life happen in such a system? If a life-friendly planet could form, it would need to accommodate diminishing temperatures. A planet like ours, in order to maintain a supply of liquid water, would have to be closer to the brown dwarf than Earth is to our Sun.

The search for invisible bodies such as brown dwarfs reflects a trend in astronomy toward examining smaller, dimmer sections of the sky. It is there, tucked into the less flashy corners of the cosmos, where life is most likely to be.

BLUE SUPERGIANT

TRIO OF BLUE SUPERGIANTS THAT FORM ORION'S BELT

MOVING UPWARD FROM THE LEFT ARE THE BRIGHT STARS ALNITAK, ALNILAM AND MINTAKA. THE HORSEHEAD NEBULA IS BELOW ALNITAK.

VISIBLE-LIGHT IMAGE

DAVID DE MARTIN WITH DATA FROM THE SAMUEL OSCHIN 48-INCH SCHMIDT TELESCOPE AT PALOMAR OBSERVATORY

1987, 1991

1,200–1,660 LIGHT-YEARS FROM EARTH

THE MOST MASSIVE AND BRILLIANT stars in the sky are blue supergiants. They are about ten times the mass of our Sun, and a few may be more than a hundred times. But these colossal stars are rare. Most stars in our galaxy are smaller than our Sun. Blue supergiants are literally one in a thousand.

Big and bright, blue supergiants stand out in the night sky. The star Rigel, for instance, in the constellation Orion has twenty times the Sun's mass and 60,000 times its brilliance. A supergiant's blue-white color and extraordinary luminance derive from its extreme surface temperature — above 55,000°F (31,000°C), compared to the Sun's surface temperature of 10,300°F (5,700°C).

But a supergiant's brilliance is short-lived by stellar standards. Burning up its gases at a furious rate, it is likely to live 10 million years, while our Sun has a 10-billion-year life span. And when a blue supergiant exhausts its nuclear fuel, it comes to a spectacular end — in a supernova. The core contracts and collapses and the outer layers crash onto it, releasing so much energy that the star is blasted apart. The collapsed core then goes on to either form a black hole or become a neutron star.

SUPERNOVA

24 SEPTEMBER 1994

10 JULY 1997

6 FEBRUARY 1998

8 JANUARY 1999

A NOVA IS A STAR THAT HAS A temporary burst of activity and increased brightness. Early astronomers, believing they were seeing a new star, used the Latin word "nova," meaning new. A supernova is a super-burst of light, but rather than a beginning it announces the cataclysmic explosion of a star at the end of its life cycle.

There are two types of supernovas. One type involves a white dwarf in a binary system with a larger star. The white dwarf pulls in matter from its companion star. When the white dwarf can no longer sustain itself it collapses, setting off a thermonuclear explosion, or supernova.

Most supernovas, however, are massive stars that have consumed all their own available fuel. In this kind of core-collapse supernova, the star's core shrinks. It gets denser and hotter — hot enough to fuse oxygen and carbon into heavier elements. Eventually, the core is solid iron, and its enormous mass causes it to collapse — in about one second. So much energy is released

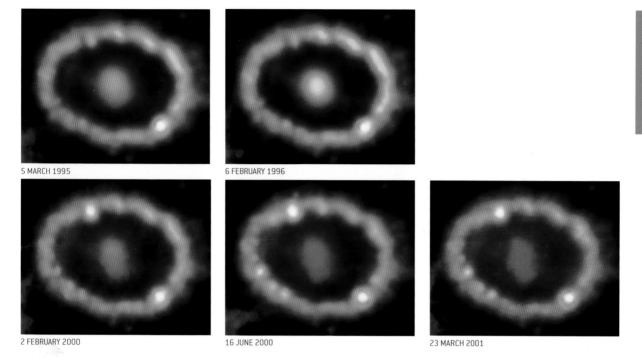

5 MARCH 1995

6 FEBRUARY 1996

2 FEBRUARY 2000

16 JUNE 2000

23 MARCH 2001

**A RING OF GAS EXCITED BY
A SHOCK WAVE FROM
SUPERNOVA 1987A IN THE
LARGE MAGELLANIC CLOUD**
(ABOVE AND FOLLOWING PAGES)

VISIBLE-LIGHT IMAGE

HUBBLE SPACE TELESCOPE
(EARTH-ORBITING)

24 SEPTEMBER 1994–
28 NOVEMBER 2003

160,000 LIGHT-YEARS
FROM EARTH

7 DECEMBER 2001

5 JANUARY 2003

that the star blasts into space. In the aftermath, the core becomes a neutron star or a black hole, depending on its mass.

Core-collapse supernovas produce incredible shock waves, sending the star's outer layers into space at speeds up to 12,500 miles (20,100km) a second. This violent ejection of matter leads to the fusion of heavy chemical elements. In fact, all elements heavier than iron in the universe were created by supernovas. These materials eventually regroup in nebulas, where new stars are born.

The images here show a ring of gaseous matter as it is illuminated by shock waves emanating from a supernova. While it was first spotted in 1987 – the brightest supernova seen from Earth in 400 years – the star actually exploded 160,000 years ago, the time it has taken for its light to reach us.

Supernovas are very rare in our galaxy. Only one supernova goes off every century in the Milky Way. But the universe is so rich in galaxies that astronomers calculate that a supernova goes off somewhere every second.

28 NOVEMBER 2003

LIGHT ECHO

When a nova flares or a supernova explodes, there is a brilliant flash of light. There is also an echo – a light echo – as the initial burst of brilliance is reflected in the neighboring dust and interstellar clouds. Over time, as the echo travels out from the star, it appears to form an expanding ring, covering a larger and larger area. This ring of light is constantly changing as it reaches and illuminates additional layers of material.

Light echoes are rare sightings. But in January 2002 a relatively dim star suddenly flared, becoming 600,000 times brighter than our Sun – temporarily the brightest star in the Milky Way.

This sequence of photographs was taken by the Hubble Space Telescope over a four-year period. They seem to show a cloud of dust expanding into space faster than the speed of light. But the cloud is not moving. What we are seeing is more and more of the surrounding cloud as it becomes illuminated by the traveling starlight. Before the Hubble's recording, the last sighting of a light echo in the Milky Way was in 1936.

A LIGHT ECHO FROM THE STAR MONOCEROTIS (V 838) IN THE CONSTELLATION MONOCEROS (ALSO FOLLOWING PAGES)

A HALO OF LIGHT APPEARS TO EXPAND AROUND A RED GIANT EXPLOSION

VISIBLE-LIGHT IMAGE

HUBBLE SPACE TELESCOPE (EARTH-ORBITING)

30 APRIL 2002– 9 SEPTEMBER 2006

20,000 LIGHT-YEARS FROM EARTH

PULSAR

In the aftermath of a supernova, if the collapsing core of the dying star has too little mass to form a black hole, it becomes a neutron star. It is left spinning furiously, its magnetic field whirling around it. As it rotates, the star sends out beams of radiation, in the form of X-rays, from its magnetic poles.

Some of these neutron stars are called "pulsars," because they emit powerful radio waves in short bursts at regular intervals — like lighthouse beams sweeping through space. Pulsars were discovered in 1967 by radio astronomers.

The pulsar in these images is the bright star in the center of the Crab Nebula, the remains of a supernova recorded by the Chinese in 1054. It sends out pulses 30 times a second.

The composite image at left shows the intense activity around the small star. The rotating pulsar generates a high-speed wind of particles that crash into the nebula, creating a shock wave that forms the inner ring. The shock sends the high-energy particles outward to form the bright outer ring. As shown in the four comparison pictures at right, both the nebula and the pulsar radiate strongly in multiple wavelengths.

A PULSAR INSIDE THE CRAB NEBULA

A SUPERNOVA REMNANT IN THE CONSTELLATION TAURUS (LEFT)

COMPOSITE OF X-RAY AND VISIBLE-LIGHT IMAGES

CHANDRA X-RAY OBSERVATORY/ HUBBLE SPACE TELESCOPE (EARTH-ORBITING)

25 NOVEMBER 2000– 6 APRIL 2001

6,500 LIGHT-YEARS FROM EARTH

MULTIWAVELENGTH COMPARISON (FOUR IMAGES AT RIGHT)

X-RAY: CHANDRA X-RAY OBSERVATORY

VISIBLE: PALOMAR OBSERVATORY

INFRARED: 2MASS

RADIO: VLA/NRAO

X-RAY

VISIBLE

INFRARED

RADIO

**CRAB NEBULA
(NGC 1952)**

THIS SUPERNOVA REMNANT
HOUSES THE PULSAR ON
THE PRECEDING PAGES. THE
ORANGE FILAMENTS ARE
THE REMAINS OF THE
STAR. THE BLUISH GLOW
IS GENERATED BY THE
PULSAR'S RAPID
SPINNING.

VISIBLE-LIGHT MOSAIC

HUBBLE SPACE TELESCOPE
(EARTH-ORBITING)

OCTOBER 1999, JANUARY
2000, DECEMBER 2000

6,500 LIGHT-YEARS
FROM EARTH

BLACK HOLE

BLACK HOLES ARE COLLAPSED pieces of our universe where time and space as we know it cease to exist. All that identifies a black hole is a remnant gravitational field that is so intense that nothing can escape once it is sucked in, even light. Today black holes are more than a theoretical curiosity. Astronomers have discovered them hidden in the cores of galaxies, and much closer to home in our galactic suburbs.

Most black holes form when a massive star runs out of fuel and explodes in a supernova. If the surviving stellar core is three times more massive than our Sun, nothing can stop it from imploding. The result is a singularity, a scrunched piece of the universe with almost no volume and infinite density. Surrounding the singularity is a boundary called the event horizon. The more massive the black hole the bigger the event horizon. But the singularity always remains smaller than the period at the end of this sentence. Anything that crosses the event horizon is trapped forever because the needed escape velocity is faster than the velocity of light – the universe's speed limit.

The term "black hole" was coined in 1967 by astronomer John Wheeler. But black holes were theorized a century before Einstein's theory of general relativity predicted the warping of space and distortion of light by gravity. In the mid-1990s, the Hubble Space Telescope confirmed the existence of black holes in the centers of galaxies by measuring the whirlpool motion of stars, dust and gas around them.

Telescopes cannot actually see material falling near an event horizon. To an outside observer, time would appear to stop – whatever is falling into the black hole would look frozen in space. This is because an intense gravitational field slows the flow of time. Hubble has viewed the onset of this effect, called a "light decay train."

An even more paradoxical idea, called "Hawking radiation" after theoretical physicist Stephen Hawking, states that black holes eventually vanish because they leak away mass in the form of particles. Empty space is constantly churning with "virtual particles" – pairs of particles with opposite charges that abruptly annihilate each other and vanish. If it happens at a black hole's event horizon, one particle might fall in before being annihilated. To conserve mass in the universe, the particle that escapes would have to be subtracted from the mass of the black hole. According to this theory, every black hole must constantly radiate energy and will eventually disappear.

In 2004 Hawking took this idea a step further by saying that information about whatever falls into a black hole – a book, a car or a breadbox – somehow survives. This means that energy flowing from a black hole actually carries information about what fell in, although in mangled form. This idea would solve a paradox from quantum theory – that information can never be destroyed in our universe.

GAS BLOWS FROM A HIDDEN BLACK HOLE AT THE CENTER OF GALAXY NGC 1068

COMPOSITE X-RAY AND VISIBLE-LIGHT IMAGE

CHANDRA X-RAY OBSERVATORY (EARTH-ORBITING)

4 DECEMBER 2000

50 MILLION LIGHT-YEARS FROM EARTH

RED GIANT

WHEN THE MAIN STAGE OF LIFE ends, all stars become red giants or – in the case of the most massive stars – red supergiants. Throughout their long and stable maturity, stars generate radiation by nuclear fusion, as heat at the core fuses hydrogen into helium. It is when the core's hydrogen is depleted that the star becomes a red giant.

At this point the core contracts, while the star itself expands, burning the hydrogen in its outer atmosphere. As the red giant grows larger, its surface cools. The core, however, contracts and becomes hotter. When the core is down to one-tenth of its former size, the temperature becomes high enough to burn helium. Nuclear fusion now resumes, and with helium fueling the core, the temperature on the surface also rises. Eventually, the helium too is exhausted.

Once the helium is gone, the most massive stars – where the core has burned intensely enough to fuse carbon and oxygen – collapse on themselves and explode, creating a supernova. This will be the fate of red supergiant Betelgeuse, shown here. One of the brightest stars in the constellation Orion, it is a thousand times the size of our Sun.

Stars the size of our Sun do not create supernovas, but their exit is surely dramatic enough. When the Sun becomes a red giant, in about five billion years, it will expand thirty or more times and become a thousand times brighter. It will consume Mercury, and possibly Venus as well. Eventually, when its helium is gone, the core will collapse into a white dwarf.

THE RED SUPERGIANT BETELGEUSE (ALPHA ORIONIS) IN THE CONSTELLATION ORION

THE FIRST DIRECT IMAGE OF A STAR'S DISK OTHER THAN THAT OF THE SUN

VISIBLE-LIGHT IMAGE

HUBBLE SPACE TELESCOPE (EARTH-ORBITING)

3 MARCH 1995

600 LIGHT-YEARS FROM EARTH

WHITE DWARF

AMONG THE DIMMEST YET HOTTEST stars in the sky are white dwarfs. These are common stars in the last stage of life. A white dwarf packs all its mass into an object a millionth its former size. On average, a white dwarf is the size of Earth, but its mass is equal to that of our Sun.

Stars of low or medium mass, like our Sun, end as white dwarfs. First, however, they become red giants. As these red giants run out of hydrogen and start burning helium, outer layers are drawn off into space, where they will form a planetary nebula. Finally, when the helium is exhausted, the core contracts into a hot, dense white dwarf.

Over time, white dwarfs will radiate away their remaining energy, growing cooler and dimmer. They may eventually become black dwarfs and disappear from view. However, since this would take many billions of years, the universe is not yet old enough for any black dwarfs to actually exist.

In this image of the Helix Nebula, a planetary nebula, an expanding circular rainbow of glowing gas surrounds a central, dying star. The speck of light in the middle is a white dwarf, which seems to float in a blue sea of gas.

THE WHITE DWARF IS THE TINY DOT IN THE CENTER OF THE HELIX NEBULA

VISIBLE-LIGHT COMPOSITE OF DIFFERENT COLOR FILTERS

HUBBLE SPACE TELESCOPE (EARTH-ORBITING)

3 NOVEMBER 2001, 19 NOVEMBER 2002

650 LIGHT-YEARS FROM EARTH

UN

GREAT
BALL
OF
FIRE

SUN

IN THE GRAND SCHEME OF THINGS, the Sun is just an ordinary, medium-size yellow star located on an arm of the Milky Way Galaxy. The Milky Way is but one of about 150 billion galaxies in the universe. Earth and seven other planets orbit the Sun. And the Sun carries them along, at 150 miles (240km) per second, as it travels on an orbit of its own within the Milky Way – a trip that takes 225 million years.

As stars go, the Sun may be no more than average size. But to us here on Earth, it is immense. One million Earths could fit into the Sun, which has a diameter of 864,000 miles (1,390,000km). It makes up 99 percent of our solar system's mass.

Life on Earth is absolutely dependent on the Sun. It is the heart of the solar system, the source of all energy, heat and light. So what would happen if the Sun suddenly shut down? Light from the Sun, which is 93 million miles (150 million km) away, travels to Earth in a matter of eight minutes. If this light were extinguished, it would take eight minutes for our world to be plunged into total darkness. Since the Sun warms our planet, all animal and plant life would be thrown into a terminal deep freeze.

SUN COMPOSITE

THREE IMAGES COMBINED TO HIGH-LIGHT DIFFERENT TEMPERATURE RANGES (SEPARATE RED, GREEN AND BLUE IMAGES ON FOLLOWING PAGES)

EXTREME-ULTRAVIOLET IMAGE (COLOR ADDED)

EIT TELESCOPE ON SOHO SPACECRAFT

92 MILLION MILES (148 MILLION KM) FROM SOHO

29 MAY 1998

93 MILLION MILES (150 MILLION KM) FROM EARTH

It is estimated that the Sun was formed 4.6 billion years ago, when our solar system was just a cloud of gas, dust and ice. Gravity caused the cloud to shrink and form into a gaseous sphere. The inner part, or center, became the Sun, while the outer part became our planets.

As our solar system evolved, Earth reached an almost solid state. The Sun, however, is still made up of gases. It is composed largely of hydrogen (92.1 percent), with some helium (7.8 percent) and a trace of heavier elements (0.1 percent).

The Sun's energy comes from nuclear fusion. Heat and pressure at the center force hydrogen atoms together. This condition starts a reaction that fuses the hydrogen nuclei and creates helium atoms. The process releases unfathomable amounts of energy and is not unlike the explosion of a hydrogen bomb.

The energy the Sun produces comes to us as light, which travels from the Sun to Earth in waves of electromagnetic radiation. And the electromagnetic spectrum contains light of every different wavelength. Some light is visible and can be seen with an optical telescope. The rest is invisible: gamma rays, X-rays, ultraviolet, infrared, microwaves and radio waves. Special telescopes can detect this invisible radiation.

But the Sun is more than a nuclear furnace, predictably

THE ULTRAVIOLET SUN

THREE IMAGES THAT HIGHLIGHT THE SUN'S TEMPERATURE RANGES (COMPOSITE ON PREVIOUS PAGE)

TOP LEFT: INNER CORONA
TOP RIGHT: LOWER INNER CORONA
BOTTOM LEFT: UPPER TRANSITION REGION BETWEEN THE CHROMOSPHERE AND THE CORONA

EXTREME-ULTRAVIOLET IMAGES (COLOR ADDED)

EIT TELESCOPE ON SOHO SPACECRAFT

92 MILLION MILES (148 MILLION KM) FROM SOHO

29 MAY 1998

93 MILLION MILES (150 MILLION KM) FROM EARTH

THE VISIBLE SUN
(BOTTOM RIGHT)

PHOTOSPHERE IN VISIBLE LIGHT

MDI TELESCOPE ON SOHO SPACECRAFT

29 MAY 1998

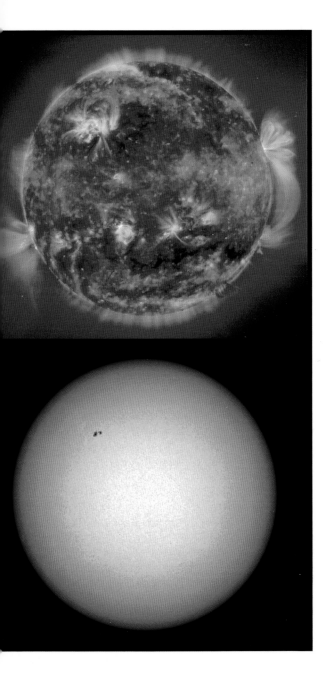

producing energy. Its sometimes erratic behavior is determined by electromagnetic activity. Like Earth, the Sun has a main magnetic field with opposite north and south magnetic poles. Earth's field is formed by the movement of molten iron within our planet's superheated core. The Sun's field is formed by the movement of electrically charged particles called plasma – a mixture of positively charged nuclei and free electrons that have been separated by the tremendous heat and radiation of the Sun's interior.

There is a cycle to the magnetic activity of the Sun. It starts with magnetic field lines (invisible lines of force) running neatly from pole to pole. But since the Sun rotates more rapidly at its equator than at its poles, the magnetic field lines tend to stretch. The flow of plasma drags these field lines about, creating new currents and producing more magnetic fields. Thus magnetic activity varies from one region of the Sun to another. Activity rises and falls. It peaks, wanes and peaks again over the course of a cycle that lasts an average of 11 years.

It is the shifting of magnetic fields that causes electrical storms in the Sun's outer atmosphere, making the corona – the halo around the Sun – hundreds of times hotter than the underlying visible surface of the Sun called the photosphere.

Magnetic field lines in the Sun's core twist and rise into the corona as loops. The volatile loops snap and reconnect with other loops, releasing energy and producing the dramatic solar events known as flares and coronal mass ejections (CMEs).

Eventually, the Sun will shut down. The hydrogen will burn out and the Sun will begin to burn helium, increasing in luminosity as well as in size. Temperatures will rise in our solar system. Once the helium is gone, the Sun will collapse into a white dwarf star the size of Earth. All this will happen in about five billion years.

CHROMOSPHERE

Derived from the Greek, chromosphere means sphere of color. This layer of the Sun's atmosphere gets its name from the faint red light it gives off, like the flickering edge of a bonfire. Normally invisible because of the glare from the Sun's surface, the chromosphere can be seen as a bright red crescent during a total eclipse.

Even though the chromosphere is 1,500 miles (2,400km) thick, it is thin by Sun standards, like patterns of ink on a printed page. The chromosphere is the outer layer of the Sun's surface, located above the photosphere and below the corona. The photosphere is the visible layer of the Sun — the part where the light that we see is emitted. Above the relatively cool photosphere, the chromosphere rises in temperature to 17,500°F (9,700°C).

The chromosphere is irregular. Narrow bursts of gas jets called spicules (right) shoot 3,000 miles (4,800km) above the surface at speeds up to 30,000mph (50,000kph).

CHROMOSPHERE
(LEFT)

ULTRAVIOLET IMAGE
(COLOR ADDED)

SUMER TELESCOPE
ON SOHO SPACECRAFT

92 MILLION MILES
(148 MILLION KM)
FROM SOHO

12 MAY 1996

SPICULES (ABOVE)

H-ALPHA,
VISIBLE-LIGHT IMAGE
(COLOR ADDED)

SWEDISH 1M
SOLAR TELESCOPE

16 JUNE 2003

93 MILLION MILES
(150 MILLION KM)
FROM EARTH

CORONA

**SOLAR CORONA
AT THE HEIGHT OF
ITS ACTIVITY CYCLE**

LOOP STRUCTURES MAP
OUT MAGNETIC FIELDS

X-RAY IMAGE
(COLOR ADDED)

YOHKOH SPACECRAFT
(EARTH-ORBITING)

1 FEBRUARY 1992

93 MILLION MILES
(150 MILLION KM)
FROM EARTH

THE CORONA, FROM THE LATIN word for crown, is the Sun's outermost layer — a roiling, blazing band of hydrogen that extends into space for millions of miles. It is typically visible to the human eye only during a solar eclipse, when it appears like a pearly halo around the edge of the Sun.

Mystery has long surrounded the workings of the corona, especially its intense heat. The corona's temperature of 3,600,000°F (2,000,000°C) greatly exceeds that of the photosphere (10,300°F/5,700°C) and the chromosphere (17,500°F/9,700°C), the two layers that lie under it, closer to the Sun's superheated core (27,000,000°F/15,000,000°C). Why is the corona so hot, when the photosphere (the 250-mile-deep/400km layer of light that we normally see) is actually closer to the Sun's core?

The extreme heat of the corona results from magnetic field lines that rise, threadlike, from the Sun's core as coronal loops. The loops carry energy through the two lower layers without effect — like smoke up a chimney flue. In the corona the loops break and reconnect, releasing charged plasma, which is converted into heat.

The corona itself is composed of three layers: an electron layer containing high-speed electrons; the dust corona, which contains slower-moving particles; and the emission line corona, which emits radiation and ultraviolet light.

Because of the corona's intense heat, its protons, neutrons and atomic nuclei move at such phenomenal speeds that many electrons are torn away in the process. As the corona's gases move away from the Sun, they become thinner and cooler, and eventually flow into interplanetary space.

CORONAL LOOP

CORONAL LOOPS
COOLING LOOPS
TWO HOURS AFTER A
SOLAR FLARE
EXTREME-ULTRAVIOLET
IMAGE (COLOR ADDED)
TRACE SATELLITE
(EARTH POLAR ORBIT)
19 APRIL 2001
93 MILLION MILES
(150 MILLION KM)
FROM EARTH

CORONAL LOOPS ARE MONUMENTAL arches of hot gases that are held in place by a strong magnetic field. The field is formed deep inside the Sun by the chaotic churning of its plasma — gases of charged particles. As the gases move about, the field becomes stronger and more buoyant and starts to rise. Eventually it balloons through the Sun's surface and becomes visible as coronal loops.

Plasma traces out the loop lines where the magnetic field is most intense. Two sunspots, one of each polarity, might form where these loops appear to perforate the surface. However, what actually happens is that both the sunspots and the loops are surrounded by an invisible portion of the field. Like magnetic highways, the invisible field constrains the gases to move along it, just as cars traveling on a highway mostly stay in their own lanes.

The loops move through the corona and connect areas of opposite polarity. They also swing back and forth, responding to the motions of the gas below the surface of the Sun. These motions lead to electrical currents that help heat the corona, just like an old-fashioned radiator heats a room.

Sometimes the currents become so large that they can no longer be contained by the field, and all hell breaks loose. The field and gas explode to eventually reorganize at a lower level of energy. As the field erupts, escaping energy can generate a violent solar flare explosion, and a gigantic plasma cloud, known as a coronal mass ejection, may be released.

CORONAL MASS EJECTION

Coronal mass ejections (CMEs) are the most dramatic and disruptive of all solar events. Created by the restructuring of magnetic fields, they are big, fast and violent. CMEs are gases of charged particles (plasma) erupting with the solar magnetic field into our Sun's upper atmosphere. And the eruptions are huge. In a matter of hours, they can grow larger than the Sun itself.

Traveling at an average speed of 300 miles (500km) per second, billions of tons of charged particles make up the bulk of a coronal mass ejection. As some of the faster CMEs expand into interplanetary space, they can create shock waves that boost charged particles in the solar wind to velocities near the speed of light.

The impact of a coronal mass ejection is somewhat like a break of billiard balls — energy is transferred from the cue ball to other balls as they're hit and speed across the table. In a CME, charged particles energize more particles in a chain reaction as they accelerate away from the Sun in a particle storm. The results can be disruptive, beautiful or fatal. For example, an astronaut can be in mortal danger if caught unaware in the path of such a storm. And if these charged particles interact with Earth's magnetic field, communications can be disrupted, or colorful light shows known as auroras can be produced in polar skies.

The filamentary structure in the image here is formed by the expansion of a coronal loop system. As the loops heat and rise, a filament lifts off and erupts as a coronal mass ejection. Both hot and cool plasma mixed with radiation are carried out into space. The cooler, heavier particles in the plasma, such as iron, can cause damage to space-based objects. However, if precautions aren't taken, the most serious effects can come from harmful radiation and from the charge buildup generated by the particle storm, which causes electronics to short-circuit.

As with other solar phenomena, such as flares and sunspots, coronal mass ejections have a cycle of about 11 years. During peak periods of magnetic activity, several eruptions can take place in a day.

A FILAMENT LIFTS OFF FROM THE SUN AND ERUPTS AS A CORONAL MASS EJECTION (RIGHT)

THE ENTIRE EARTH COULD EASILY FIT INTO THE ARMS OF THIS 75,000-MILE-HIGH (121,000KM) SOLAR STRUCTURE

EXTREME-ULTRAVIOLET IMAGE (COLOR ADDED)

TRACE SATELLITE (EARTH POLAR ORBIT)

19 JULY 2000

93 MILLION MILES (150 MILLION KM) FROM EARTH

A CORONAL MASS EJECTION BLASTS BILLIONS OF TONS OF PARTICLES AT MILLIONS OF MILES PER HOUR (FOLLOWING PAGES)

THE YEARS 2000 AND 2002 DOUBLE-PEAKED AS PERIODS OF HIGH ACTIVITY KNOWN AS THE SOLAR MAXIMUM

COMPOSITE OF THE CORONA (VISIBLE LIGHT) BY LASCO C2 INSTRUMENT AND THE CENTRAL SUN (EXTREME ULTRAVIOLET) BY EIT TELESCOPE, BOTH ON SOHO SPACECRAFT

92 MILLION MILES (148 MILLION KM) FROM SOHO

7 AUGUST 2002

AURORA

Auroras are the biggest and most spectacular light shows in Earth's atmosphere — beautiful but potentially dangerous spectacles. Like fireworks over Shanghai on the Chinese New Year or Rio de Janeiro during Carnival, brilliant and changing colors paint parts of the sky.

Named for the Roman goddess of dawn, auroras usually appear in the skies above the Earth's North and South poles — named respectively the aurora borealis or northern lights and the aurora australis or southern lights. While they seem to be mirror images of each other, there are significant differences in timing, intensity and location.

Auroras occur when electrons and protons from coronal mass ejections are propelled through space and crash into atoms in a planet's upper atmosphere. Something electric happens there. As the solar particles collide with the planet's oxygen and nitrogen atoms, the particles give up some of their energy to the atoms. As they return to normal, the atoms give

AURORA BOREALIS

ULTRAVIOLET IMAGE
OF THE AURORA OVERLAID
ON A VISIBLE-LIGHT
IMAGE OF EARTH

AURORA: NASA POLAR
SPACECRAFT
EARTH: TERRA AND
DMSP SATELLITES

17 SEPTEMBER 2000

AURORA: 34,000 MILES
(54,000KM) FROM
POLAR SPACECRAFT

EARTH: 150 MILES (241KM)
BELOW AURORA

off energy in the form of colorful glowing light. The energy from the solar particles also wreaks havoc with satellites and terrestrial power grids.

An aurora's colors depend on what atoms are struck by electrons at what height. Green lights result from oxygen emissions at 60 miles (100km). At higher altitudes oxygen emissions produce red lights. Neutral (un-ionized) nitrogen produces pink lights, while ionized nitrogen creates the rare blue or violet lights.

The lights typically adorn the cold skies above our polar regions. Auroras follow Earth's magnetic field lines, which direct the energetic electrons to the auroral oval, the area that encircles each pole. Auroras have also been observed on other planets, including Saturn and Jupiter. Auroras occur on these planets because they have powerful magnetic fields and atmospheres that can be electrified by charged particles.

**AURORA BOREALIS AND
AURORA AUSTRALIS
ON SATURN**

AURORAL CURTAINS
AT POLES RISE 1,000 MILES
(1,600KM) ABOVE CLOUDS

ULTRAVIOLET IMAGE

HUBBLE SPACE
TELESCOPE
(EARTH-ORBITING)

OCTOBER 1997

810 MILLION MILES
(1.3 BILLION KM)
FROM EARTH

SUNSPOT

SUNSPOT GROUP NEAR SOLAR CENTER (LEFT)

VISIBLE-LIGHT IMAGE (COLOR ADDED)

SWEDISH 1M SOLAR TELESCOPE

14 AUGUST 2003

93 MILLION MILES (150 MILLION KM) FROM EARTH

SUNSPOT IN ACTIVE REGION 10030 (FOLLOWING PAGES)

VISIBLE-LIGHT IMAGE (COLOR ADDED)

SWEDISH 1M SOLAR TELESCOPE

15 JULY 2002

A SUNSPOT LOOKS LIKE A BLACK patch on the Sun's luminous, visible surface, the photosphere. However, the dark spot is not totally devoid of light.

Sunspots happen where the Sun's magnetic field suppresses light and heat from the area it surrounds. When giant bundles of magnetic field lines emerge from inside the Sun as coronal loops, their imposing presence inhibits the flow of heat. These spots punctuate where the field is strongest, resulting in a cooler surface area — apparent in visible-light images as a sunspot. The middle of the spot, called the umbra, looks black because it is a thousand or more degrees cooler than the neighboring photosphere, which is about 10,000°F (5,500°C).

There is an average 11-year sunspot cycle that is influenced by the Sun reversing its overall magnetic polarity. If a compass could survive on the Sun, the needle would switch from north to south. During this period, the number of visible sunspots goes from a maximum to a minimum and back to a maximum again. At the height of the cycle, 150 sunspots may be visible in a single sunrise-to-sunset period. Sunspots often appear in pairs of opposite magnetic polarity.

FLARE

Flares are violent outbursts of energy and matter that occur around sunspots, causing a sudden radiance. They are the biggest explosions in the solar system. Plasma in the Sun's atmosphere is heated to tens of millions of degrees, and charged hydrogen particles accelerate to near the speed of light. Flares emit radiation and shock waves that can last from minutes to hours.

Scientists theorize that flares are released when the Sun's magnetic field lines tear and reconnect, expelling a large amount of magnetic energy into the corona. According to Dr Brian R. Dennis, astrophysicist at the Goddard Space Flight Center, the largest solar flares are energetically equivalent to 100 billion times the size of the atomic bomb dropped on Hiroshima.

Flares follow the solar cycle of magnetic activity that spans an 11-year period of high and low intensities. When the cycle is at its peak, flares increase in frequency and force.

Flares and coronal mass ejections (CMEs) often occur together, suggesting there may be a connection. But while the energized particles from flares tend to be confined to the solar vicinity, the CME particles — moving away from the Sun at near the speed of light — go off into interplanetary space.

CMEs are believed to be the main source of high-energy charged particles that pose dangers to astronauts traveling to the Moon or Mars. But the relationship between flares and CMEs is not fully understood. Considerable research is now under way due to safety concerns about the impact of these gigantic solar events on future space projects.

FLARE

THE WHITE HORIZONTAL LINE IS AN ABERRATION CAUSED BY THE INTENSE BRIGHTNESS OF THE FLARE

EXTREME-ULTRAVIOLET IMAGE (COLOR ADDED)

EIT TELESCOPE ON SOHO SPACECRAFT

92 MILLION MILES (148 MILLION KM) FROM SOHO

4 NOVEMBER 1997

93 MILLION MILES (150 MILLION KM) FROM EARTH

PROMINENCE

A PROMINENCE IS A BRIGHT GAS cloud arching outward from the Sun. The term encompasses different types of clouds and flamelike structures that are rooted in the chromosphere and expand into the corona. These ghostly shapes commonly have lower temperatures and higher densities than their surroundings. When such structures are viewed rising over the edge of the Sun, they appear bright and are known as prominences. When viewed against the background of the Sun's bright disk, they appear

SOLAR PROMINENCES

COLLAGE OF 4
EXTREME-ULTRAVIOLET
IMAGES (COLOR ADDED)

EIT TELESCOPE
ON SOHO SPACECRAFT

92 MILLION MILES
(148 MILLION KM)
FROM SOHO

DATES (CLOCKWISE
FROM UPPER LEFT):
15 MAY 2001,
28 MARCH 2000,
18 JANUARY 2000,
2 FEBRUARY 2001

93 MILLION MILES
(150 MILLION KM)
FROM EARTH

dark and are known as filaments.

Think of a prominence as an explosion at a gas station, spewing smoke and flame. The gaseous plumes might be compared to what is known as active prominences. Found in areas of flares and sunspots, active prominences are dynamic, moving in a whirling motion. They can look like a loop, spray or surge shooting tens of thousands of miles off the Sun's surface.

There are other kinds of prominences. Eruptive prominences derive from the same violent origins as coronal mass ejections (charged particles that are expelled when magnetic field lines break and resplice to each other). In fact, many coronal mass ejections are accompanied by eruptive prominences.

Prominences categorized as quiescent are stable structures, lasting weeks or even months, that develop away from the Sun's active regions and along magnetic neutral lines. Quiescent prominences can extend 30,000 miles (50,000km) above the Sun's surface.

ECLIPSE

On occasion, a celestial body is hidden from view because another body moves in front of it. At other times, a celestial body becomes hidden by the shadow of another. These events are called eclipses.

A solar eclipse occurs when the Moon passes between Earth and Sun and blocks the Sun's light from arriving in some area on Earth. In a total solar eclipse, the entire Sun is blocked out and only a faint halo of light, the corona, is visible. If the Moon covers only part of the Sun, it is called a partial solar eclipse.

When the Earth blocks the Sun's light from the Moon, it is known as a lunar eclipse. A total lunar eclipse occurs when the Moon passes completely through the Earth's shadow. But in a total lunar eclipse, the Moon rarely disappears. Instead, it typically turns red. This results from a small amount of light that reflects off Earth, bends or refracts and then bounces off the Moon. In a partial lunar eclipse, the Moon passes through only a part of the Earth's shadow.

Eclipses are actually happening all the time. In theory, they can be observed anytime and anywhere because they are driven by the location of the observer. For example, if a celestial body passes between you and a star, then you are witnessing an eclipse.

TOTAL ECLIPSE OF THE SUN BY THE MOON SHOWS STREAMERS OF THE SOLAR CORONA

MOON ILLUMINATED BY SUNLIGHT REFLECTED FROM EARTH

COMPOSITE OF 22 VISIBLE-LIGHT IMAGES

FRED ESPENAK WITH 90MM REFRACTING TELESCOPE

11 AUGUST 1999

238,868 MILES (384,403KM) FROM EARTH TO MOON

ECLIPSE
OF THE SUN
BY EARTH

THIS RARE PHOTOGRAPH CAPTURES an eclipse of the Sun by Earth, a phenomenon that is observable only from space. In this case, the eclipse was recorded by the crew of Apollo 12 on its return to Earth from the Moon in November 1969. As the trajectory of the spacecraft placed it within Earth's shadow, Earth eclipsed or blocked the Sun.

At the time, the crew members were focused on reentering Earth's atmosphere. So when Mission Control asked them to photograph the passing event, the astronauts had to move quickly to respond. According to Captain Alan Bean, they wasted no time calculating exposures. They bracketed the exposures and "hoped something would turn out." Indeed it did. The astronauts are the only humans ever to have seen, let alone record, an eclipse of the Sun by Earth.

**ECLIPSE OF SUN BY EARTH
AS SEEN FROM SPACE**

VISIBLE-LIGHT IMAGE

HANDHELD 70MM
HASSELBLAD

APOLLO 12

24 NOVEMBER 1969

30,000 MILES (48,000KM)
FROM APOLLO 12 TO EARTH

PLAN

NETS

FOLLOW
THAT
STAR

JUPITER'S NORTHERN HEMISPHERE (LEFT)

NEAR TRUE-COLOR MOSAIC OF 36 IMAGES

CASSINI ORBITER

12.5 MILLION MILES (20 MILLION KM) FROM CASSINI

11, 12 DECEMBER 2000

380 MILLION MILES (611 MILLION KM) FROM EARTH

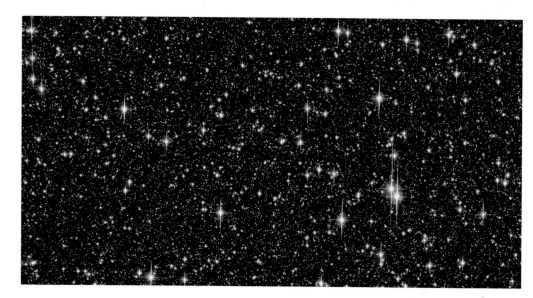

PLANET

PLANETS ARE THE MOST EXPLORED and sought after objects in the universe. That's because we live on a planet. The more planets we find out there, the less likely it is that we are alone in the universe. So far, more than 200 have been discovered orbiting other stars. And more and more are found every year.

The word planet is from the ancient Greek for "wanderer." The earliest sky watchers were intrigued by five bright pinpoints of light that moved freely against the background of stars.

Close-up views of the planets from spacecraft are unveiling worlds of much more complexity, diversity and dynamism than once imagined. Today we know

that the planets are intimately intertwined because they share a common birth. They all formed out of a pancake-shaped disk of dust and gas that encircled our newborn Sun 4.5 billion years ago. Their evolutionary fate was determined by many factors – including their size and distance from the Sun.

For example, the terrestrial planets (Mercury, Venus, Earth and Mars) which are closest to the Sun are rocky, because intense solar heat burned off most of their gas. Farther out, where it's colder and where gas could survive, the less dense gas giants (Jupiter, Saturn, Uranus and Neptune) took shape. Farther out and colder still, icy bodies formed – among them, the dwarf planets Pluto and the newly named

Eris, formerly known as Xena.

Discoveries in our solar system and elsewhere have forced astronomers to reconsider the definition of a planet. A planet not only must orbit a star, but also must have been born in a disk of debris swirling around the star (this rules out stellar companions, such as brown dwarfs, that are too far from their stars to have formed in a disk). The planet must also be large enough to have sufficient gravity to pull itself into a spherical shape (this rules out most asteroids). Finally, a planet must dominate its orbit so that it does not share its region of space with other bodies (this rules out Pluto, which lies in a belt among other icy bodies).

Our galaxy may have a far more exotic variety of planets.

16 EXO-PLANETS HAVE BEEN FOUND IN THIS CROWDED CENTRAL REGION OF THE MILKY WAY (ABOVE)

VISIBLE-LIGHT IMAGE

HUBBLE SPACE TELESCOPE (EARTH-ORBITING)

22–29 FEBRUARY 2004

26,000 LIGHT-YEARS FROM EARTH

We know of some the size of Jupiter that migrate so close to their parent star that they complete an orbit in less than ten hours, and are so hot that their atmospheres are boiling away. It is even suggested that there exist "carbon planets," with volcanoes spewing out diamonds over a tarry landscape.

PLANET-FORMING DISK

THE BIRTH OF PLANETS OFTEN accompanies the birth of stars. A star is born inside a dense nebular cloud of gas and dust. As the star forms, a flat, dusty disk gathers around it in which planets may be born. The disk starts out as a primary proto-planetary disk and evolves to a secondary debris disk. Both disks are known as circum-stellar disks.

This planet-forming disk, composed of tiny grains of matter, is the beginning of a solar system. The grains in the inner disk, where rocky planets form, consist mostly of magnesium, silicon and iron. The grains in the outer disk, where gas giants take shape, are thousands of times more plentiful and are composed mostly of ices — water, ammonia and methane.

These bits collide at low speeds and stick together. As bodies of a mile or more in diameter form, their gravitational pull becomes strong enough to attract more material at an ever increasing rate. In a

FACE-ON VIEW OF THE DEBRIS DISK AROUND THE STAR HD 107146 (BLACKED OUT IN CENTER) (ABOVE)
LARGE GAS PLANETS MAY ALREADY EXIST IN THE DISK. ROCKY, EARTHLIKE PLANETS MAY BE JUST STARTING TO FORM.
VISIBLE-LIGHT IMAGE
HUBBLE SPACE TELESCOPE (EARTH-ORBITING)
5 JUNE–20 JULY 2004
88 LIGHT-YEARS FROM EARTH

PROTOPLANETARY DISKS SURROUND INFANT STARS (RED-PINK) IN THE SERPENS STAR-FORMING REGION (RIGHT)
INFRARED IMAGE
SPITZER SPACE TELESCOPE (EARTH-TRAILING SOLAR ORBIT)
5, 6 APRIL 2004
848 LIGHT-YEARS FROM EARTH

**A PLANET-FORMING DEBRIS DISK
AROUND AU MICROSCOPII**
(RIGHT)

THE SPINDLE-SHAPED OBJECT
IS AN EDGE-ON DISK IN THE
FINAL STAGES OF PLANET
FORMATION AROUND A NEWBORN STAR
(BLACK GAP IN CENTER)

VISIBLE-LIGHT IMAGE

HUBBLE SPACE TELESCOPE
(EARTH-ORBITING)

3 APRIL 2004

33 LIGHT-YEARS FROM EARTH

few million years, a full-blown
planet can emerge.

As evolving planets, comets
and asteroids circle the star in
the primary disk, they crash
into one another and shatter.
The debris from the impact gathers to form a giant doughnut-
shaped disk. The center of this
secondary disk may be carved
out by orbiting planets. Over
time the debris clears, leaving
a smaller and more stable disk,
similar to the Kuiper Belt in our
own outer solar system.

In 2004, the Hubble Space
Telescope photographed two
such secondary debris disks.
The face-on disk on page 138
encircles the Sun-like star HD

107146, which is between 50 and 250 million years old. The red dwarf star at left, AU Microscopii, is only 12 million years old and is surrounded by a disk seen edge on. Both show gaps in the disk where planets may have removed dust and cleared a path.

One nearby incubator for young planets is a star-forming region located in the direction of the constellation Serpens the Snake (page 139). Precise measurements from the Spitzer Space Telescope reveal an excess of infrared light coming from the young stars. They are illuminating the clouds of gas around them. Spitzer can't

resolve the small disks, but their telltale infrared glow is evidence of protoplanetary disks. Wisps of green throughout the image indicate the abundance of carbon-rich molecules, the elements of planet formation.

Located only 60 light-years away, the sunlike star Beta Pictoris (above) was the first one ever discovered with a planet-forming dust disk. It was detected in 1983 by its infrared glow. This Hubble Space Telescope image represents the sharpest view ever of the nearly edge-on disk. The disk extends outward to about ten times the distance of Pluto from the Sun.

Warps in the disk may be

caused by the presence of planets disturbing the dust with their gravity. Additional evidence for planets comes from recent Hubble images that actually reveal two disks, one slightly inclined to the other. The disk system has an inner gap, about the width of our solar system, where planets may have already formed. The star's age is estimated at a few hundred million years, and so the disk is much richer in dust than seen around older stars like our Sun.

EDGE-ON VIEW OF TWO CIRCUMSTELLAR DUST DISKS AROUND BETA PICTORIS (BLACK IN CENTER) (ABOVE)

THE SECONDARY DISK IS AT A 4° INCLINE FROM THE PRIMARY DISK, SLANTING UPWARD FROM LEFT TO RIGHT. THE COLORFUL SPIKY RAYS AND SPECKLED BACKGROUND ARE ARTIFACTS.

VISIBLE-LIGHT IMAGE

HUBBLE SPACE TELESCOPE (EARTH-ORBITING)

1 OCTOBER 2003

63 LIGHT-YEARS FROM EARTH

MERCURY

MERCURY

MOSAIC OF VISIBLE-
LIGHT IMAGES

MARINER 10
SPACECRAFT

125,000 MILES
(201,000KM) FROM
MARINER 10

MARCH 1974–
MARCH 1975

48–138 MILLION MILES
(77–222 MILLION KM)
FROM EARTH

MERCURY IS THE PLANET CLOSEST to the Sun and the fastest in the solar system. Named for Mercurius, the Roman god of speed, commerce and travel, Mercury races through space at a mean speed of 30 miles (48km) a second, circling the Sun along an elliptical path in just 88 Earth days.

In contrast to its speedy orbit, Mercury's rotation around its axis is extremely slow: 59 Earth days. One rotation on Mercury, however, is not equal to one day. From sunrise to sunrise, one day lasts much longer – 176 Earth days. In fact, one Mercury day lasts two Mercury years.

This is so because the period of Mercury's rotation is linked to the period in which Mercury orbits the Sun. Mercury rotates one and a half times during each orbital period, naturally increasing the length of a day.

If one were positioned on the planet surface watching the Mercury sky, this strangeness could be experienced. At some point during the day, the Sun would seem to slide back and forth. It would come to a complete stop, move backward for a while and then progress back to the original stop position before moving on. At certain longitudes, a person would actually see a double sunrise and a double sunset due to this phenomenon.

Mercury's elliptical orbit carries it as close as 29 million miles (46 million km) to the Sun and as far as 43 million miles (70 million km). This huge variation in distance and the fact that a year is shorter than a day would make the size of the Sun seem to change dramatically during one daytime period.

Mercury's temperature fluctuations are also the most extreme in the solar system, a result both of the planet's proximity to the Sun and the absence of a protective atmosphere. Temperatures on the "day" or Sun side of the planet can soar as high as 801°F (427°C); on the "night" side, they can plummet to −279°F (−173°C). With no atmosphere to protect its surface, Mercury also has no defense against meteorites; like Earth's Moon, much of its surface is scarred by impact craters from collisions with meteors.

Mercury has no moons of its own, and until recently was thought to have no water. In 1991, astronomers studying the planet using radar reported that Mercury may have water ice at its north pole. The evidence exists deep inside craters where the Sun does not shine.

VENUS

EXCEPT FOR OUR SUN AND OUR Moon, Venus is the brightest object in our sky, easily visible with the naked eye. The Romans named it after the goddess of love and beauty.

Venus is an inner rocky planet, situated between Mercury and Earth. Because Venus is close to Earth in size, mass, composition and distance from the Sun, it is considered a kind of twin to Earth. But it is a far different world from ours. Venus is hot – the hottest planet in the solar system, with a surface temperature of about 900°F (480°C). Venus is even hotter than Mercury, the planet closest to the Sun.

Venus has no oceans, rain or wind. It has a thick atmosphere of spinning clouds that trap surface heat. This cloud layer produces a greenhouse effect, making it hot enough to melt lead. The clouds also reflect sunlight, which accounts for Venus's luminosity. The planet has no satellites and no magnetic field to speak of.

VENUS

COLOR-CODED MOSAIC
OF RADAR IMAGES

MAGELLAN SPACECRAFT

182 MILES (294KM)
FROM MAGELLAN

SEPTEMBER 1990–
SEPTEMBER 1992

24–162 MILLION MILES
(38–261 MILLION KM)
FROM EARTH

Another dramatic difference from Earth is the intense pressure of the Venusian atmosphere. Its surface pressure is 90 times that of Earth, so standing on Venus would feel as if you were 3,000 feet (900m) deep in an ocean here on Earth. The dense atmosphere is composed primarily of carbon dioxide, droplets of sulfuric acid and almost no water vapor. The intense surface pressure is why probes that have landed on Venus have survived only hours before being crushed.

Venus's rotation is slow and a little strange. It rotates on its axis only once every 243 Earth days. Most unusual is the planet's retrograde or "backward" rotation. Venus spins in the opposite direction of its orbit around the Sun, which would make the Sun seem to rise in the west and set in the east. Venus orbits the Sun every 225 Earth days, but its retrograde rotation means that a day on Venus lasts 117 Earth days.

VENUS SCAPES

IN DETAILED CLOSE-UPS, THE
topography of Venus seems
almost familiar. Like Earth,
Venus has a relatively young
surface. It consists mainly of
rolling upland plains, with some
lowlands and highlands. There
are volcanoes, too, although
none appears to be active today.

   Altogether, there may be
more than a million volcanoes
or volcanic centers larger than
half a mile (1km) in diameter
and more than 1,000 volcanoes
larger than 12 miles (20km).
Much of the planet's surface is
covered in lava flow. In the
northern highlands, the Ishtar
Terra is a lava-filled basin larger
than the continental United
States. And along the equator,
the Aphrodite Terra highlands
extend for 6,000 miles
(10,000km), half the size of
Africa. While there are large
impact craters on Venus, there
are few small ones because
the dense atmosphere burns
up most meteors before they
reach the surface.

AKNA MONTES (MOUNTAINS)
WITH THE 14-MILE-WIDE (22KM)
IMPACT CRATER WANDA (LEFT)

THE 43-MILE-WIDE (69KM) IMPACT
CRATER DICKINSON, IN VENUS'S
ATALANTA REGION (RIGHT)

RADAR IMAGES

MAGELLAN SPACECRAFT

182 MILES (294KM)
FROM MAGELLAN

1990–1992

24–162 MILLION MILES
(38–261 MILLION KM)
FROM EARTH

VENUS TRANSIT

IN ASTRONOMICAL TERMS, A transit is the passing of a planet across the face of a star. It is a rare occurrence, and of the two transits visible from Earth, Mercury and Venus, that of Venus is rarer. Mercury passes in front of the Sun an average of 13 times every century. Venus's transits occur in widely separated eight-year pairs, at alternating intervals of 105.5 and 121.5 years.

Since the invention of the telescope in 1610, there have been seven transits of Venus: in 1631, 1639, 1761, 1769, 1874 and 1882. The most recent transit occurred in June 2004 and took approximately six hours to complete. The event was visible from start to finish in Europe, Africa and Asia, but not from the Western Hemisphere. The next transit will take place in June 2012.

Astronomers used to be interested in Venus's transits as a means of calculating the distance between Earth and the Sun. Now transits are used to search for other planetary systems. When a planet passes across its central star, there is a momentary reduction in the star's luminosity. By studying such reductions, scientists hope to pinpoint the location and confirm the existence of still unidentified planets in unknown solar systems.

VENUS IN TRANSIT ACROSS THE SUN

VISIBLE-LIGHT IMAGE THROUGH H-ALPHA FILTER

STEFAN SEIP WITH 100MM F/8 APOCHROMATIC REFRACTING TELESCOPE

8 JUNE 2004

26.9 MILLION MILES (43.2 MILLION KM) FROM EARTH TO VENUS AT THE DATE OF TRANSIT

94.4 MILLION MILES (151.9 MILLION KM) FROM EARTH TO SUN AT THE DATE OF TRANSIT

EARTH

THE GREEK WORD FOR LAND IS "ge" or "ga." Gaia was the goddess of the Earth. She was born from the vast emptiness of the universe called Chaos. Viewed from space, Earth distinguishes itself: Set against a black canvas are blue waters, brown-green land masses and white clouds. But what is truly unique about Earth is that as far as astrobiologists can determine, this is the only planet in our solar system where life exists.

Earth is one of eight planets in a solar system located on a spiral arm of the Milky Way Galaxy. It is the third planet from the Sun – an average distance of 93 million miles (150 million km) – and one of the four terrestrial planets in the inner solar system. The fifth largest planet, Earth has one satellite, the Moon.

If Earth is ordinary in size and location, it is extraordinary because of its water and its air. It is the only planet where water exists in abundance and where there is an atmosphere that can support many life forms. Water is the foundation of all life on Earth, and Earth is the only known planet where water exists in all three states: solid, liquid and gas. In liquid form, water covers more than 70 percent of the planet's surface. And even though we know the oceans by names such as the Atlantic and the Pacific, Earth really has just one big ocean.

Powerful forces of wind and water combine to regulate the climate worldwide. They help keep Earth's temperature relatively stable. Winds create daily weather patterns. Oceans have

TRUE-COLOR MOSAIC OF EARTH
TERRA SATELLITE (EARTH-ORBITING)
438 MILES (705KM) FROM TERRA
JUNE–SEPTEMBER 2001

a slower, longer-lasting effect on climate change. The Northern Hemisphere contains most of Earth's land. As a result, it heats and cools quickly, which makes for hotter summers and colder winters. The Southern Hemisphere, by contrast, has more water, which heats and cools more slowly, bringing milder weather with fewer extremes of temperature.

Earth's atmosphere is a layer of gases that surrounds and assists the planet. As a vehicle for our cycle of water, clouds in the atmosphere redistribute water from oceans to land in the form of precipitation. These gases also usefully serve to keep radiation from the Sun both in and out. In a process called the greenhouse effect, gases such as carbon dioxide entrap infrared radiation, thus making the planet warm enough for life to spread. In Earth's upper atmosphere a layer of gaseous ozone (molecules of oxygen with three atoms) acts as a natural sunblock, protecting us from most of the Sun's harmful ultraviolet radiation.

Our atmosphere consists of 78.1 percent nitrogen and 20.9 percent oxygen, the gas we need to breathe. The remaining 1 percent is water vapor and other gases, including carbon dioxide. It is all held together, like almost everything else, by gravity. Ninety-nine percent of the mass of Earth's atmosphere is in the first 40 to 50 miles above the surface. The gases become thinner and thinner with increasing elevation. At about 37,000 miles (60,000km), the atmosphere ends.

High above our atmosphere

is a protective shield known as the magnetosphere. Earth is like a huge magnet, which creates our magnetosphere, an invisible magnetic bubble surrounding the planet. The magnetosphere protects Earth by deflecting high-energy ejections from the Sun, which are moving through space at speeds that often exceed a million miles an hour. These ejections of charged particles could destroy life if they all reached Earth's surface. Occasionally some particles break through the magnetosphere and are channeled along invisible lines of force toward the polar regions. When they hit the atmosphere, they sometimes cause it to glow, creating the famous northern and southern lights.

Earth is the densest body in our solar system. It is made up of several layers: the crust, the upper mantle, the lower mantle,

RICHAT STRUCTURE, SAHARA DESERT, MAURITANIA

THIS DOME OF LAYERED SEDIMENTARY ROCKS IS OFTEN NOTED BY ASTRONAUTS FROM SPACE

LANDSAT IMAGE DRAPED OVER AN ELEVATION MODEL FROM THE SHUTTLE

LANDSAT SATELLITE (EARTH-ORBITING) SHUTTLE RADAR TOPOGRAPHY MISSION

437 MILES (703KM) FROM LANDSAT 145 MILES (233KM) FROM THE SHUTTLE

13 JANUARY 1987 (LANDSAT) 11–22 FEBRUARY 2000 (SHUTTLE)

an outer core and an inner core. The crust is a solid layer of rock that forms continents and seabeds. Earth's crust is thinner under the oceans and thicker on land. Most of Earth's mass is contained in its mantles. The upper mantle is hot molten rock, the lower mantle more solid. While Earth's outer core is liquid, the inner core is a solid ball of mostly iron, about the size of Mars. Temperatures at Earth's center are hot — hotter than the Sun's surface.

Earth's surface is young. The crust and upper mantle are broken into seven large and many smaller tectonic plates. Because the upper mantle is hot and moldable, the plates can slide around, spreading apart from and colliding with each other. This shifting causes earthquakes and volcanic eruptions. Most earthquakes occur at the edges of tectonic plates, along fault lines or fractures in the crust. The movement of plates (along with wind and

LAVA FLOWS ON THE SOUTHERN FLANK OF MOUNT ETNA (RIGHT)

VISIBLE-LIGHT IMAGE WITH INFRARED LAVA FLOWS

TERRA SATELLITE (EARTH-ORBITING)

438 MILES (705KM) FROM TERRA

29 JULY 2001

water erosion) reshapes the surface over time; for example, mountains were formed by buckling crust.

Earth is 4.6 billion years old. There are no records of its formative geology or of the organisms that may have lived in the very beginning. We do know that life started in single cells and then multiplied. Scientists have identified about 1.8 million species living today, most of them in the oceans. But the life forms that we see today represent only a small proportion of those that have existed on planet Earth. Over time, most of the species that ever lived – an incredible 99 percent – have died out.

OLDUVAI GORGE, TANZANIA
(LEFT)

THE GORGE (THE FAINT HORIZONTAL LINE NEAR THE CENTER) IS NOTED FOR EARLY HOMINID FOSSILS

DIGITAL ELEVATION MAP

SHUTTLE RADAR TOPOGRAPHY MISSION

145 MILES (233KM) FROM THE SHUTTLE

11–22 FEBRUARY 2000

JUNCTION OF THE AMAZON AND RIO NEGRO RIVERS AT MANAUS, BRAZIL
(FOLLOWING PAGES)

VISIBLE-LIGHT AND NEAR-INFRARED IMAGE

TERRA SATELLITE (EARTH-ORBITING)

438 MILES (705KM) FROM TERRA

16 JULY 2000

MARS

WITH ITS RED HUE AND PROXIMITY to Earth, Mars has fascinated us across the centuries. It is the fourth planet in our solar system and the last of the rocky planets orbiting close to the Sun. The Babylonians associated the planet with war and bloodshed. So did other civilizations – the Romans named Mars for their god of war.

The astronomer Giovanni Schiaparelli observed strange markings on the planet in 1877. He called them "canali," which means channels in Italian but was translated incorrectly as "canals." This sparked the Victorian misconception that Mars was populated by an alien race of innovative canal builders who irrigated the planet with melting ice from the polar caps.

By the early 1970s, a world of unimagined diversity revealed itself to the orbiting eyes of the Mariner 9 spacecraft: towering volcanoes, immense rift valleys, and a cobweb of dried river channels eerily reminiscent of Schiaparelli's illusory canals. This made it clear that Mars had an interesting geologic history that may take decades to unravel.

The focus of current exploration has been water. Water is so important because it offers the tantalizing possibility of life as we understand it. An armada of NASA and ESA orbiters, landers and rovers are beginning to explore every nook and cranny looking for traces of water.

Within the past eight years, new gullies — bright patches carved into flowing shapes in the Martian dust — have appeared within two craters. The gullies likely carried five to ten swimming pools' worth of briny water down the crater slopes. This implies that there is liquid water near the surface of Mars today. It may hide in aquifers, frozen ice or snow packs.

In 2004, the Mars Exploration Rovers (MERs) Spirit and Opportunity found proof of past liquid water in various surface features. The bedrock of Gusev Crater indicates an ancient body of salt water. Evidence of a body of water larger than the Baltic Sea exists in the Terra Meridiani region. "Every single rock has shown signs of alteration by liquid water," said lead investigator Dr Steven Squyres.

Three-dimensional images released from the Mars Express spacecraft in early 2005 show evidence of past gigantic waterfalls, huge glaciers and grand outflow channels. Near the equator, along the Elysium Plains, one photograph shows what appears to be a five-million-year-old frozen sea of water that has been protected from vaporizing by a layer of volcanic ash. Comparable in size and depth to the North Sea, the area features large irregular

A DAY ON MARS

COMPUTER-GENERATED SPHERE MADE FROM 24 VISIBLE-LIGHT IMAGES

MARS GLOBAL SURVEYOR ORBITER

230 MILES (370KM) FROM THE ORBITER (AVERAGE)

10–11 APRIL 1999

62 MILLION MILES (100 MILLION KM) FROM EARTH

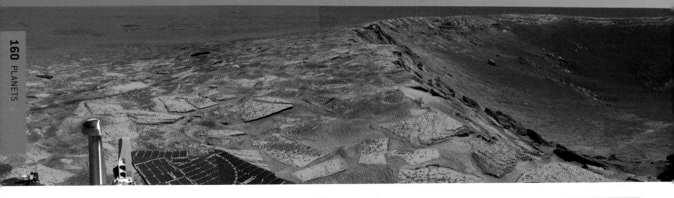

plates similar in pattern to the pack ice at Earth's poles.

Following the water trail away from the sea leads to a series of fissures known as the Cerberus Fossae. These fractures in the surface were the source of both lava and water floods millions of years ago. In fact, lava plains from the floods are located in eastern Elysium.

The find is captivating because on Earth microorganisms have been found around deep-sea thermal vents. If the Elysium seawater was warmed by past geothermal energy, perhaps it provided the environment for life to develop in a similar form on Mars.

The recent detection of small amounts of methane in the Martian atmosphere is further intriguing evidence for living microorganisms on the planet. Methane is a common byproduct of life on Earth, but it can also be produced by non-biological processes. Volcanoes could be one source, but there is no proof of active volcanism on Mars today. Still, all other

ENDURANCE CRATER IN MERIDIANI PLANUM REGION (TOP)

APPROXIMATE TRUE-COLOR MOSAIC PANORAMA MADE OVER SEVEN SOLS (MARTIAN DAYS)

VISIBLE-LIGHT IMAGE

MARS EXPLORATION ROVER OPPORTUNITY

CRATER DIAMETER IS 427 FEET (130M)

23–29 MAY 2004

218 MILLION MILES (350 MILLION KM) FROM EARTH

SELF-PORTRAIT OF OPPORTUNITY IN SHADOW INSIDE ENDURANCE CRATER (RIGHT)

VISIBLE-LIGHT IMAGE

26 JULY 2004

31.5 FEET (9.6M) FROM OPPORTUNITY TO TIP OF SHADOW

243 MILLION MILES (391 MILLION KM) FROM EARTH

MICROSCOPIC VIEW INSIDE EAGLE CRATER IN MERIDIANI PLANUM REGION (LEFT)

IRON-RICH PEBBLES SHOW EVIDENCE OF PAST WATER

VISIBLE-LIGHT IMAGE

4 INCHES (100MM) FROM OPPORTUNITY

16 FEBRUARY 2004

143 MILLION MILES (230 MILLION KM) FROM EARTH

possible causes must be ruled out before concluding that methane is a biotracer of present-day life on the planet.

The atmosphere on Mars is thin, composed mainly of carbon dioxide gas. There are clouds, mist and fog, but the atmosphere lacks the insulation to prevent wide temperature swings, as much as 180°F (100°C) from day to night.

If water flowed on Mars, perhaps billions of years ago, it must have been at a time when the atmosphere was much denser. Because of the current tenuous atmosphere, water on Mars behaves like carbon dioxide on Earth: Frozen water doesn't melt; it goes directly from ice to vapor without an intervening liquid state. This process, known as sublimation, poses a dilemma for scientists in explaining what appears to be considerable erosion on the surface.

The main reservoir of water on the planet is concentrated in the ice at the north and south poles, although enormous quantities of water ice may exist underground at low latitudes.

Mars is now entombed in a global ice-age cold. Surface temperatures average −65°F (−53°C) and even during the summer rarely rise above the freezing point of water (32°F/ 0°C). Variations in temperature across the surface produce strong winds, often stirring massive summer dust storms that engulf the planet. Summers are warmer and shorter in the southern hemisphere than in the north because of Mars's pronounced elliptical orbit.

The Martian hemispheres are a mismatched pair. The southern terrain is more ancient and heavily cratered, with obvious valley networks possibly

NORTH POLAR LAYERS OF ICE-RICH DEPOSITS EXPOSED IN A CLIFF WALL AT CHASMA BOREALE (LEFT)

THE PATTERN OF FRACTURES NEAR THE TOP IS PROBABLY DUE TO WATER ICE IN THE DEPOSITS. THE DARKER MATERIAL BELOW MAY HAVE BEEN DEPOSITED AS SAND DUNES.

VISIBLE-LIGHT IMAGE (FALSE COLOR)

MARS RECONNAISSANCE ORBITER

198 MILES (317KM) FROM ORBITER

8 NOVEMBER 2006

239 MILLION MILES (384 MILLION KM) FROM EARTH

A FROZEN SEA NEAR THE EQUATOR IS THOUGHT TO BE PROTECTED FROM VAPORIZING BY A COATING OF VOLCANIC ASH (RIGHT)

THE TWO IMPACT CRATERS WERE FORMED BEFORE THE AREA WAS FLOODED. RUBBLE PILES AROUND THE CRATERS PROVIDED CLUES TO A FROZEN SEA.

VISIBLE-LIGHT IMAGE (NEAR TRUE COLOR)

MARS EXPRESS

162 MILES (260KM) FROM MARS EXPRESS

19 JANUARY 2004

118,380 MILLION MILES (190,505 MILLION KM) FROM EARTH

**POSSIBLE PROOF OF
LIQUID WATER ON MARS
IN A CRATER IN THE
CENTAURI MONTES REGION**

THE GULLY DEPOSIT
AT RIGHT FIRST APPEARED
IN FEBRUARY 2004.
THE DEPOSIT EXHIBITS
CHARACTERISTICS OF
LIQUID WATER.

MARS GLOBAL
SURVEYOR ORBITER

230 MILES (370KM)
FROM THE ORBITER
(AVERAGE)

LEFT:
30 AUGUST 1999
109 MILLION MILES
(176 MILLION KM)
FROM EARTH

RIGHT:
10 SEPTEMBER 2005
57 MILLION MILES
(92 MILLION KM)
FROM EARTH

formed by past rivers. Along the equator is Valles Marineris. Grander than the Grand Canyon, it is a system of deep canyons that spans an extraordinary 2,500 miles (4,000km). This is a relic from a time when the crust of Mars stretched a little, but did not trigger full-scale plate tectonics as on Earth.

Evidence for lack of plate tectonics can be found in the huge Tharsis Plateau in the northern hemisphere. Here volcanoes dot the landscape of the younger plains. Elevation is lower and the surface is markedly smooth, showing indications of former lake beds. The north's most imposing feature, Olympus Mons, is the largest volcano in our solar system — a hundred times larger than Mauna Loa, the largest on Earth.

The border between these two geologically dissimilar hemispheres hints at traces of an ancient coastline from a possible northern ocean — one bigger than the combined size of the Mediterranean Sea and Arctic Ocean. It would have been up to a mile deep in water, covering about one-sixth of the planet.

The changing seasons of Mars, its ice caps, clouds, volcanoes and canyons— all make for similarities with Earth. But that is where the similarity ends. Mars is rocky, cold and barren. It has two moons, Phobos (meaning fear) and Deimos (meaning panic). The entire Martian planet is about the size of Earth's iron core. The planet's red color is derived from the presence of olivine and iron oxide on its surface. It is as if the whole intriguing planet is coated in rust.

ROVER OPPORTUNITY SUPERIMPOSED ON THE EDGE OF VICTORIA CRATER TO GIVE A SENSE OF SCALE (ABOVE)

THE DRAMATIC PROMONTORY KNOWN AS CAPE VERDE WAS PHOTOGRAPHED BY OPPPORTUNITY AT 165 FEET (50M) FROM THE ROVER

VISIBLE-LIGHT IMAGE

MARS EXPLORATION ROVER

28 SEPTEMBER 2006

243 MILLION MILES (391 MILLION KM) FROM EARTH

OPPORTUNITY APPEARS AS A SMALL SPECK ON THE RIM OF VICTORIA CRATER IN THE 10 O'CLOCK POSITION (FAR RIGHT)

VISIBLE-LIGHT IMAGE (COLOR ENHANCED)

MARS RECONNAISSANCE ORBITER

3 OCTOBER 2006

106 MILLION MILES (171 MILLION KM) FROM EARTH

DETAIL OF MAIN IMAGE WITH OPPORTUNITY AS A BLUE DOT AT TOP CENTER (NEAR RIGHT)

FIVE DAYS BEFORE THIS IMAGE WAS TAKEN, OPPORTUNITY ARRIVED AT VICTORIA CRATER AFTER A 5-MILE (9-KM) DRIVE FROM MERIDIANI PLANUM

AFTERWARD, THE ROVER MOVED TO THE VERY EDGE OF CAPE VERDE TO PHOTOGRAPH THE INTERIOR OF THE CRATER

WITH A CAREFUL LOOK, ONE CAN SPY THE ROVER'S TRACKS

**KASEI VALLIS,
ONE OF THE LARGEST
CHANNELS ON MARS,
CARVED BY GLACIERS
OR WATER-RELATED
OUTFLOWS** [RIGHT]

VISIBLE-LIGHT IMAGE
[NEAR TRUE COLOR]

MARS EXPRESS

169 MILES [272KM]
FROM MARS EXPRESS

29 JANUARY 2004

127 MILLION MILES
[204 MILLION KM]
FROM EARTH

**OVERHEAD VIEW OF THE
CYDONIA REGION**
[ABOVE]

THIS AREA IS KNOWN
FOR THE "FACE ON MARS,"
FIRST PHOTOGRAPHED
BY VIKING 1 IN 1976.
THE FACE CAN BE SEEN
FAINTLY BELOW CENTER.

VISIBLE-LIGHT IMAGE
[NEAR TRUE COLOR]

MARS EXPRESS

202 MILES [325KM]
FROM MARS EXPRESS

22 JULY 2006

228 MILLION MILES
[368 MILLION KM]
FROM EARTH

**IMPACT CRATER ON
VASTITAS BOREALIS,
A BROAD PLAIN THAT
COVERS MUCH OF
THE FAR NORTHERN
LATITUDES**
[FOLLOWING PAGES]

THE BRIGHT CIRCULAR
PATCH AT CENTER IS
RESIDUAL WATER ICE

VISIBLE-LIGHT IMAGE
[NEAR TRUE COLOR]

MARS EXPRESS

198 MILES [318KM]
FROM MARS EXPRESS

2 FEBRUARY 2005

189 MILLION MILES
[303 MILLION KM]
FROM EARTH

**A CHANNEL IN
TINJAR VALLIS
(VALLEY) CARVED
BY WATER OR
VOLCANIC LAVA
(LEFT)**

20 OCTOBER 2002

235 MILLION MILES
(378 MILLION KM)
FROM EARTH

**KNOBS AND
MESAS IN ATLANTIS
CHAOS REGION
PROBABLY FORMED
BY EROSION
(BOTTOM)**

30 MAY 2002

232 MILLION MILES
(373 MILLION KM)
FROM EARTH

**A CRATER IN THE
POLAR REGION
SURROUNDED
BY SEDIMENTARY
ROCK OR
VOLCANIC ASH
(NEAR RIGHT)**

18 NOVEMBER 2003

55 MILLION MILES
(89 MILLION KM)
FROM EARTH

**OLIVINE-RICH BED-
ROCK (MAGENTA
TO PURPLE-BLUE)
IN THE AREA OF
SYRTIS MAJOR
(FAR RIGHT)**

THE ABUNDANCE
OF OLIVINE, WHICH
DECOMPOSES EASILY
WHEN WET, INDI-
CATES AN ANCIENT
DRY PAST

30 MARCH 2002–
14 JUNE 2004

213 MILLION MILES
(343 MILLION KM)
FROM EARTH

FAR RIGHT IMAGE:
INFRARED MOSAIC
(FALSE COLOR)

OTHER 3 IMAGES:
VISIBLE LIGHT
(COLOR ENHANCED)

ALL 4 IMAGES:
THEMIS INSTRUMENT
ON 2001 MARS ODYSSEY
SPACECRAFT
(MARS-ORBITING)

249 MILES (400KM)
FROM ODYSSEY
TO MARS
(MEAN ALTITUDE)

**THE CENTRAL AREA
OF VALLES MARINERIS
CANYON, WHICH
IS LARGER THAN THE
GRAND CANYON
IN THE U.S.
(FOLLOWING PAGES)**

SULFATE MINERALS FOUND
IN LAYERS OF SEDIMENT
INDICATE PAST WATER
ACTIVITY IN THE CANYON

VISIBLE-LIGHT MOSAIC
(NEAR TRUE COLOR)

MARS EXPRESS

24 APRIL 2004,
2 MAY 2004

326 MILES (525KM),
466 MILES (750KM)
FROM MARS EXPRESS

200 MILLION MILES
(325 MILLION KM)
FROM EARTH

ASTEROID

ASTEROID EROS

21 MILES (33KM) LONG,
8 MILES (13KM) WIDE
AND 8 MILES THICK

A MOSAIC OF VISIBLE-LIGHT
AND INFRARED IMAGES
DRAPED OVER A
COMPUTER MODEL
OF THE ASTEROID SHAPE

NEAR SHOEMAKER PROBE

124 MILES (200KM)
FROM NEAR SHOEMAKER

29 FEBRUARY 2000

160 MILLION MILES
(258 MILLION KM)
FROM EARTH

ASTEROIDS ARE SPACE RUBBLE, dark rocky fragments created during the formation of the solar system almost five billion years ago. This orbiting debris is the leftover material that didn't quite come together to make a planet or a moon.

Asteroids come in irregular shapes and sizes. Some are larger than the length of Italy, while others are less than a few city blocks in diameter.

Most asteroids orbit the Sun in the gap between Mars and Jupiter, which is known as the Asteroid Belt. Asteroid orbits are usually stable for millions of years. However, because asteroids are so small and there are so many of them, their orbits are not confined to a single, ecliptic plane like those of planets. Asteroid orbits span a large range of inclinations due to the long-term effects of the gravitational pull of Jupiter, Mars, or nearby asteroids.

While tumbling through space, have asteroids ever hit Earth? It is believed that a huge asteroid or comet slammed into what is now the Yucatan peninsula 65 million years ago. Asteroid hits are rare, but mete-oroid hits occur almost continu-ally, adding tons of material to our planet every day. Meteoroids are often the offspring of aster-oids or comets.

JUPITER

JUPITER
A TRUE-COLOR MOSAIC
OF 27 IMAGES
CASSINI ORBITER
6.2 MILLION MILES
(10 MILLION KM)
FROM CASSINI
29 DECEMBER 2000
391 MILLION MILES
(629 MILLION KM)
FROM EARTH

NAMED AFTER THE ROMAN GOD OF all gods, Jupiter is the largest planet in the solar system. Second in brightness after Venus as viewed from Earth, Jupiter could be filled with a thousand Earths. Yet it measures only one-tenth of the Sun's diameter.

The planet is like a bustling metropolis, with many satellites, a colorful ring system, turbulent storms and streaks of lightning. Like the hub of a great city – Times Square in New York or the Ginza in Tokyo – Jupiter is big, bright and commanding.

In 1610, Galileo discovered Jupiter's four largest moons – Io, Europa, Ganymede and Callisto – now called the Galilean satellites. Today we know that Jupiter has at least 63 satellites – the most of any

planet in the solar system. Many of the outer moons may be asteroids caught by the planet's intense gravity.

Jupiter is one of the four gas giants, along with Saturn, Neptune and Uranus. In composition, Jupiter is similar to a star. In fact, the gas giant sends out into space more than one-and-a-half times the heat it receives from the Sun. Yet, even with all the right stuff, Jupiter falls short of the weight requirement for a star to ignite. The planet needs about eighty times more mass for fusion to commence in its core.

Even though Jupiter has no solid surface, its designation as a gas giant is strangely misleading. The majority of the planet is made of hydrogen

under such supersize pressure that it has turned liquid and metallic. Jupiter is divided into four main layers: a thin outer envelope of gaseous hydrogen, a deep sea of liquid hydrogen, a deeper sea of liquid hydrogen acting like molten metal, and a hot core of ice and rock.

Jupiter has a strong magnetic field generated by electrical currents deep in the planet's liquid metallic hydrogen layer. Within the magnetic field there is an abundance of charged particles. These particles create dangerous radiation, which bombards Jupiter's rings and moons. The planet's strong magnetic field interacts with the solar wind to create a magnetic tail that extends as far as Saturn's orbit.

JUPITER'S GREAT RED SPOT

JUPITER'S MOST NOTABLE FEA-ture may be its Great Red Spot, a huge storm system more than 12,500 miles (20,000km) wide, about twice the width of Earth. It is, in fact, the largest storm in our solar system. And it has been there, in Jupiter's southern hemisphere, for at least 350 years, since English naturalist Robert Hooke first reported it. But it is now only half as big as it was a century ago.

The Great Red Spot is a vortex of high and cool clouds driven by strong winds of up to 250mph (400kph). Scrunched in between two jet streams in the upper atmosphere, the mass of clouds twirl upward and rotate counterclockwise every six days. It is anticyclonic –

that is, a high-pressure system, unlike the low-pressure cyclonic hurricanes on Earth. Storms like this one last so long on the gas giants because there are no solid surfaces below to break them up.

Along with smaller cloud systems that act like thunder-storms, the Great Red Spot is located in Jupiter's kaleidoscop-ic cloud lanes. As pictured on the previous pages, the lighter bands are rising gases called zones, while the darker bands are descending gases called belts. Perpetual strong winds, steady alternating jet streams and the fast rotation of the plan-et (a day is under ten hours) – all contribute to these atmo-spheric stripes.

**JUPITER'S
GREAT RED SPOT**

VISIBLE-LIGHT IMAGE

VOYAGER 2

3.7 MILLION MILES
(6 MILLION KM)
FROM VOYAGER 2

3 JULY 1979

500 MILLION MILES
(805 MILLION KM)
FROM EARTH

JUPITER: THE RINGS

JUPITER'S RING SYSTEM (THE horizontal lines in the photograph) was first discovered in 1979 by NASA's Voyager 1 spacecraft. We now know that the planet's ring is made up of three major sections.

The main ring, approximately 4,000 miles (6,500km) wide, is encircled by the orbits of two small moons, Adrastea and Metis. Its inner border merges into the faint and thickest ring, called the halo. This doughnut shape extends halfway from the main ring to Jupiter's cloud tops and may be caused by the electrical charging of particles that spiral inward. Neighboring the main ring on the outside is a pair of faint gossamer rings. One of the pair is contained by the orbit of the moon Amalthea and the other by the moon Thebe. The gossamers are thicker than the main ring due to the inclined path of the two moons as they circle Jupiter.

The Jovian ring system is highly tenuous and uniform, composed of tiny dust particles a few microns in diameter. Astronomers speculate that the rings may be formed by dust kicked up as interplanetary meteoroids smash into the planet's inner moons — Metis, Adrastea, Amalthea and Thebe.

RING SYSTEM TO THE LEFT AND RIGHT OF A BACKLIT JUPITER (ABOVE)

COMPOSITE OF TWO MOSAICS IN VISIBLE LIGHT

RINGS: GALILEO ORBITER ARCS OUTLINING JUPITER: VOYAGER 2

1.4 MILLION MILES (2.3 MILLION KM) FROM GALILEO

RINGS: 9 NOVEMBER 1996 ARCS: 1979

500 MILLION MILES (805 MILLION KM) FROM EARTH

CLOUD CIRCULATION IN JUPITER'S NORTHERN HEMISPHERE

LIGHT BLUE CLOUDS ARE HIGH AND THIN, REDDISH CLOUDS ARE DEEP AND WHITE CLOUDS ARE HIGH AND THICK

NEAR-INFRARED MOSAIC

GALILEO ORBITER

870,000 MILES (1.4 MILLION KM) FROM GALILEO

3 APRIL 1997

500 MILLION MILES (805 MILLION KM) FROM EARTH

THE CLOUDS

MUCH LIKE A STAR, JUPITER'S gaseous atmosphere is about 90 percent hydrogen and 10 percent helium. Floating above the gases is the visible cloud layer. Composed of ammonia (NH_3) ice crystals, the colorful shell is many miles thick and very turbulent, with no solid surface beneath. The clouds result from hotter temperatures at lower altitudes causing ammonia to well up from the interior. As the ammonia rises into colder and higher altitudes, it freezes and forms the clouds. The billowing marbled coloration is probably caused by chemical contaminants.

Giant lightning flashes have been detected by both the Voyager and Galileo probes. The lightning occurs in anticyclonic regions where turbulence is formed by abruptly changing winds traveling from north to south. The source of these electrical discharges may be water-ice clouds located at a lower altitude.

SATURN

"WHEN WE HAVE ACTUALLY SEEN that great arch swung over the equator of the planet without any visible connection, we cannot bring our minds to rest," wrote a Saturn-struck James Clerk Maxwell in the 1850s.

The ringed planet continues to fascinate as the most exotic in our solar system. It is also the second largest – 75,000 miles (120,700km) in diameter – and the most distant planet easily visible to the naked eye.

The hundreds of thin, wide rings can be seen with a small telescope. They change in appearance relative to the tilt and position of Earth and Saturn, sometimes opening wide, other times narrowing to almost nothing edge on. They consist of billions of particles of ice and rock, caught in the planet's gravity as in a fisherman's net, then sent spinning in a majestic hula hoop. Although the other gas giants also have orbiting rings, Saturn's are the biggest and the brightest. With the exception of the Cassini Division (an expanse of 2,900 miles/4,600km), they are relatively close to one another, reinforcing the halo

SATURN IN NATURAL COLOR

VISIBLE-LIGHT MOSAIC OF 126 IMAGES
CASSINI ORBITER
3.9 MILLION MILES
(6.3 MILLION KM) FROM CASSINI
6 OCTOBER 2004
0.9 BILLION MILES
(1.4 BILLION KM) FROM EARTH

effect as viewed from Earth.

Named for the father of the god Jupiter, Saturn has at least 33 moons, most discovered since 1980. The largest, Titan, is bigger than Mercury. Saturn spins on its axis in just 10 hours and 15 minutes, but due to its distance from the Sun — nearly a billion miles (1.6 billion km) — Saturn takes 30 times as long as Earth to complete its orbit.

One of the four gas giants, Saturn is composed mainly of hydrogen and helium gases, with a hot rocky core and a south pole that amazingly is the warmest place on the planet. Atmospheric pressure is sufficient to cause Saturn's gases to condense into a slush of liquid hydrogen about 250 miles (400km) below the cloud tops. The planet's density is the lowest in the solar system, its specific gravity less than that of water; if there were an ocean large enough to contain it, the planet would float.

The atmosphere is composed of three layers of clouds — white, orange and blue — and capped with a thick layer of haze. Storms more forceful than Jupiter's occasionally climb through the haze and appear as white clouds of ammonia ice. Winds in the upper atmosphere reach speeds as high as 1,100 mph (1,800kph) as they whirl around the equator. The winds, in combination with the heat rising from the planet's interior, account for the yellow and gold

bands visible in Saturn's atmosphere. The synergy of high-speed rotation and the planet's gaseous makeup produces its characteristic flat poles and a bulging equator, the plumpest in the solar system.

In 2004, after a two-billion-mile, seven-year journey, the Cassini-Huygens spacecraft entered Saturn's orbit to give the planet its close-ups.

MONOCHROMATIC MOON DIONE AGAINST SATURN'S MULTIHUED CLOUD BANDS (LEFT)

VISIBLE-LIGHT IMAGE

CASSINI ORBITER

499,000 MILES (803,000KM) FROM CASSINI TO DIONE

22 SEPTEMBER 2005

0.9 BILLION MILES (1.45 BILLION KM) FROM EARTH

SATURN'S NIGHT SIDE AGAINST THE SHINING B AND C RINGS (BELOW)

SATURN'S SOUTHERN HEMISPHERE LIT BY SUNLIGHT REFLECTING OFF THE RINGS

VISIBLE-LIGHT MOSAIC OF 126 IMAGES

CASSINI ORBITER

900,000 MILES (1.4 MILLION KM) FROM CASSINI

28 SEPTEMBER 2006

0.93 BILLION MILES (1.5 BILLION KM) FROM EARTH

DIONE

IAPETUS

TETHYS

MIMAS

TITAN

A
SAMPLER
OF
SATURN'S
MOONS

ENCELADUS

PHOEBE

HYPERION

RHEA

THE MOON MIMAS AGAINST SATURN'S NORTHERN HEMISPHERE
(RIGHT)

SHADOWS OF THE RINGS STREAK SATURN'S SURFACE. THE BRIGHT BLUE STREAK ABOVE MIMAS IS SUNLIGHT PASSING THROUGH THE CASSINI DIVISION. THE TRANSPARENT A RING APPEARS AT THE BOTTOM.

VISIBLE-LIGHT IMAGE

CASSINI ORBITER

2.3 MILLION MILES (3.7 MILLION KM) FROM CASSINI

7 NOVEMBER 2004

0.8 BILLION MILES (1.3 BILLION KM) FROM EARTH

**THE MOON PAN
SWEEPS AWAY DUST IN
THE ENCKE GAP**

VISIBLE-LIGHT IMAGE

CASSINI ORBITER

484,000 MILES
(779,000KM)
FROM CASSINI TO PAN

16 DECEMBER 2006

0.8 BILLION MILES
(1.3 BILLION KM)
FROM EARTH

RINGS AND MOONS
(RIGHT)

THREE OF SATURN'S
MOONS BEYOND THE
F RING — JANUS (TOP),
PANDORA (CENTER)
AND MIMAS (BOTTOM)

VISIBLE-LIGHT IMAGE

CASSINI ORBITER

1.7 MILLION MILES
(2.7 MILLION KM)
FROM CASSINI

22 JANUARY 2005

0.75 BILLION MILES
(1.2 BILLION KM)
FROM EARTH

SATURN: THE RINGS

SATURN'S RINGSCAPE IS LIKE A mini-solar system where the planet, moons and ring particles are balanced in a collaborative display. The inner satellites play a key role as they choreograph particles to clear gaps, create waves and form ringlets.

Even though there are a multitude of ringlets, the ring plane is divided into seven main rings designated by letters — D, C, B, A, F, G and E in order

outer portion of the A ring and is formed by the orbital path of the tiny moon Pan. Pan acts like a rotating broom sweeping away debris as it moves through the gap, causing ropelike braids and wakes along Encke's edges.

Satellites Prometheus and Pandora perform a different role by shepherding the F ring into a narrow strand. Prometheus is on the inside of the ring, Pandora on the outside. The gravitational

PANORAMA OF RINGS (BELOW)

VARIATIONS, GAPS, GRAVITATIONAL RESONANCES AND WAVE PATTERNS ARE REVEALED IN SATURN'S MOST STRIKING FEATURE

VISIBLE-LIGHT MOSAIC

CASSINI ORBITER

1.1 MILLION MILES (1.8 MILLION KM) FROM CASSINI

12 DECEMBER 2004

PASTEL-COLORED SATURN EMBRACED BY THE SHADOW OF ITS RINGS (RIGHT)

THE SUBTLE NORTH-WARD GRADATION FROM GOLD TO AZURE IS NOT FULLY UNDERSTOOD

VISIBLE-LIGHT IMAGE

CASSINI ORBITER

621,000 MILES (999,000KM) FROM CASSINI

4 MAY 2005

0.87 BILLION MILES (1.4 BILLION KM) FROM EARTH

from the planet. The closer rings orbit Saturn at faster speeds. Density waves within the rings are the result of nearby passing moons. The revolving moons disturb the orbits of particles, and density waves are formed as particles move closer together.

The Cassini Division between the B and A rings is the largest apparent interruption in Saturn's grooves. The inner boundary is formed by particles located on the outer edge of the B ring. They orbit Saturn twice for every time the moon Mimas goes around the planet once. This process is called orbital resonance.

One of the smaller gaps, the Encke Division, is located in the

forces of the moons corral any material trying to escape.

There's little consensus about how long the Saturnian ring system has been in place and how long it might last. The rings are evolving dynamically such that over the next few hundred million years, the outer parts may fall toward the planet and the structure collapse. The fact that we see the rings today means that there must be some sort of renewal process — perhaps the shattering of moons — that rebuilds the rings. It is most unlikely that the rings have existed only for a brief period of time in the solar system's 4.5-billion-year history.

THE SUN BEHIND SATURN HIGHLIGHTS THE OUTLINE OF THE SPHERE AND THE RING PLANE (FOLLOWING PAGES)

LIGHT FROM THE RINGS IS REFLECTED IN THE SOUTHERN HEMISPHERE. EARTH CAN BE SPOTTED AS A PALE DOT TO THE LEFT OF SATURN AND ABOVE THE BRIGHT RINGS.

VISIBLE-LIGHT MOSAIC OF 165 IMAGES

CASSINI ORBITER

1.3 MILLION MILES (2.2 MILLION KM) FROM CASSINI

15 SEPTEMBER 2006

0.92 BILLION MILES (1.5 BILLION KM) FROM EARTH

URANUS

URANUS AND SATELLITES
(ABOVE)

NEAR-INFRARED IMAGE

EUROPEAN SOUTHERN
OBSERVATORY,
8.2M VLT ANTU
TELESCOPE

19 NOVEMBER 2002

1.9 BILLION MILES
(3 BILLION KM)
FROM EARTH

URANUS WITH RINGS
(OPPOSITE)

NEAR-INFRARED IMAGE
(ENHANCED COLOR)

HUBBLE SPACE TELESCOPE
(EARTH-ORBITING)

8 AUGUST 1998

1.8 BILLION MILES
(2.8 BILLION KM)
FROM EARTH

"ON THE VOYAGER PROJECT, WE used to call Uranus a featureless blue tennis ball," says planetary scientist Dr Ellis D. Miner. "In fact, it is anything but."

Uranus, the third largest planet in the solar system and seventh from the Sun, was identified as a comet by British astronomer William Herschel in 1781. Others (including his son) were the first to recognize that it was a new planet. The rings, however, were not discovered for another two centuries.

Named for the Greek god of the heavens, Uranus has 11 rings, some of the brightest clouds at the far edge of the solar system and 27 known moons. Most moons were named for Shakespearean characters, including Portia, Cordelia, Oberon and Puck. Miranda (the heroine of THE TEMPEST) features steep cliffs and winding valleys that scientists think may be evidence of the partial melting of the moon's interior.

Uranus is a gas giant with no solid surface. Eighty percent of its mass consists of a liquid core made up mainly of icy materials (water, methane and ammonia). Hydrogen, helium and a small quantity of methane make up its atmosphere. Methane gas above the cloud layers of its upper atmosphere gives the planet a distinctive blue-green color.

In 2004, observations conducted at the W.M. Keck Observatory in Hawaii identified at least 31 cloud features that changed quite dramatically between viewings. These cloud features are massive storms that could encompass a nation the size of the United States. The clouds, at varying altitudes, are probably made of methane crystals that condense as gas bubbles during their rise from deep in the atmosphere.

Perhaps most interesting is the unique polar orientation of this planet. Uranus orbits the Sun with its axis nearly horizontal to the ecliptic plane, like a top spinning on its side. A collision with a planet-size body early in its life probably explains its tipped rotation, which results in the two poles of this very cold planet receiving the greatest exposure to the Sun in the course of a long orbit of 84 years.

NEPTUNE

**NEPTUNE WITH ITS
GREAT DARK SPOT,
A HURRICANELIKE
STORM** (TOP LEFT)

VISIBLE-LIGHT IMAGE

VOYAGER 2

4.4 MILLION MILES
(7 MILLION KM)
FROM VOYAGER 2

21 AUGUST 1989

3 BILLION MILES
(4.8 BILLION KM)
FROM EARTH

**NEPTUNE'S
SOUTH POLE**
(MAIN IMAGE)

VISIBLE-LIGHT IMAGE

VOYAGER 2

20 AUGUST 1989

NAMED AFTER THE ROMAN GOD OF the sea, the gas giant Neptune is now considered the most distant planet, a vast 2.8 billion miles (4.5 billion km) away from the Sun.

Neptune was the first planet discovered as a result of mathematical calculation rather than astronomical observation. Studying irregularities in the motion of Uranus, scientists posited the gravitational pull of a larger, then unknown, planet.

Because of Neptune's distance from the Sun, its orbit takes 165 years. That means the planet has not yet completed a full circle since its discovery in 1846. The distance also makes it impossible to see with the naked eye.

Neptune and Uranus are essentially twins in size. Neptune is slightly smaller in diameter but slightly larger in mass. Neptune's interior is also similar to its twin – composed of the melted ices of water, methane and ammonia, with a rocky core about the size of Earth. Hydrogen, helium and methane gas make up its atmosphere. The methane absorbs red from the illuminating sunlight, giving Neptune its blue color. And the planet's winds are strong, the fastest in the solar system.

Neptune has a ring system and 13 known moons. Triton is not only the largest of Neptune's moons, but it is also the largest moon in the solar system with a retrograde orbit.

PLUTO

PLUTO IS THE ONLY PLANET DISCOV-ered in the 20th century and the only one ever found through a photographic survey. The search for a planet beyond Neptune was inaugurated in 1915 because astronomer Percival Lowell erroneously thought that an unseen body was perturbing Neptune's orbit. The search continued after Lowell's death. Lowell Observatory astronomer Clyde Tombaugh discovered Pluto in 1930. It was named after the Roman God of the underworld, and also begins with Lowell's initials, P.L. Early estimates were that it was the size of Earth. But Pluto can be called the "incredible shrinking planet" because estimates grew smaller with each successive discovery.

Today we know that finding Pluto was a remarkable achievement, like finding a needle in a haystack. Astronomers had to wait for advanced instrumentation in the 1990s before other Pluto-like bodies were found in the same outer zone of the solar system. Pluto is among the largest members of the Kuiper Belt, a swarm of icy debris left behind from the early days of the solar system. In 2006, another Kuiper Belt object, called Eris, was found to be 5 percent bigger. This helped lead the International Astronomical Union (IAU) to reclassify Pluto as a "dwarf planet" in 2006.

A companion object to Pluto was discovered in 1978. Half the size of Pluto, it was named Charon after the boatman of the river Styx in Roman mythology. The Pluto-Charon system is sometimes considered a double planet because they orbit a common center of gravity.

In 2005 the Hubble Space Telescope discovered two more satellites around Pluto, named Nix and Hydra. These small bodies are believed to be in nearly circular orbits. If they were captured objects, they would most likely be in elliptical orbits. This means that they were probably formed from a titanic collision between Pluto and another Kuiper Belt object. This same crash perhaps gave birth to Charon as well. Nix and Hydra appear to orbit in the same plane as Charon — strong evidence for a common birth.

About two-thirds the diameter of our Moon, Pluto may be composed of a rocky core surrounded by an icy mantle. This is much like the composition of the moons of the outer planets, especially Neptune's Triton.

Pluto takes 248 years to circle the Sun. It is in a peculiar orbit, which is gravitationally influenced by Neptune. Pluto plays a kind of cat-and-mouse game with Neptune. For a 20-year period during its long, elliptical orbit, Pluto is actually closer to the Sun than Neptune is. The last time that Pluto was in close orbit to the Sun was from 1979 to 1999.

Unlike Earth, where the seasons are determined by the planet's tilt, Pluto's seasons are driven by its distance from the Sun. Its orbit carries it as close as 2.5 billion miles (4.3 billion km) and as far away as 4.4 billion miles (7.4 billion km).

During Pluto's recent summer, temperatures were a balmy −378°F (−228°C). Ground-based telescopes measured an increase in gaseous methane as the thin atmosphere warmed and grew puffier. Hubble images show a variegated surface with bright patches of methane frost, and darker areas where the methane coating perhaps vaporized to uncover a darker terrain.

As Pluto moves away from the Sun and moves into winter, its atmosphere will probably freeze onto the surface, coating it with fresh methane frost. The white frost may also increase Pluto's reflecting power, lowering temperatures even faster.

No craft has ever visited Pluto, but NASA's New Horizons mission is heading that way at a speed of 50,000 miles (80,000km) per hour. Even at that velocity it will not reach Pluto until 2015.

PLUTO (LEFT) WITH ITS THREE MOONS

CHARON IS PLUTO'S BIGGEST MOON (LOWER RIGHT). NIX AND HYDRA ARE THE TWO PINPOINTS OF LIGHT AT FAR RIGHT.

VISIBLE-LIGHT IMAGE

HUBBLE SPACE TELESCOPE (EARTH-ORBITING)

15 FEBRUARY 2006

2.9 BILLION MILES (4.7 BILLION KM) FROM EARTH

COMET

COMET C/2001 Q4 (NEAT)
(ABOVE)

VISIBLE-LIGHT COMPOSITE
THROUGH RED, GREEN
AND BLUE FILTERS

WIYN 0.9M TELESCOPE
AT KITT PEAK NATIONAL
OBSERVATORY, NOAO

7 MAY 2004

29.7 MILLION MILES
(47.9 MILLION KM)
FROM EARTH

The gas, meanwhile, dissipates into space. The atoms of gas lose some electrons, and the remaining electrons move to a higher energy level due to the effects of sunlight and vacuum conditions. The resulting gas atoms (ions) that are positively charged are pulled along by the solar wind and fluoresce as the outer remaining electrons fall back to lower energy levels. To remote observers, the fluorescence is visible as a distinct ion tail that is often blue in color and up to a hundred million miles long.

The abundance of comets, and their random paths into the solar system, suggest that they originate in a "comet reservoir" called the Oort Cloud. This hypothetical shell of trillions of comet nuclei lies about one light-year from our Sun. Many other comets come from the much closer Kuiper Belt, a ring of icy bodies that encircle the Sun and stretch out from the orbit of Neptune to about three billion miles (4.5 billion km) from the Sun.

COMETS ARE BASICALLY LEFTOVERS from the formation of our solar system. Irregular balls of ice, dust, rocks and gas just a few miles wide, comets move in long elliptical orbits that bring them close to the Sun either repeatedly (as with Halley's 76-year orbit) or rarely.

A comet's most prominent feature is its dust tail, although comets sometimes form a secondary tail, called an ion tail. The tails generally begin to form when the comet approaches within a few hundred million miles of the Sun. The Sun heats a comet's nucleus, causing ice to vaporize and turn to gas that is explosively expelled along with a lot of dust. The dust forms a huge coma or head around the nucleus, often reaching thousands of miles in diameter. As sunlight exerts radiation pressure on the dust particles, they slowly drift away from the coma, forming the comet's bright dust tail.

SCHWASSMAN-
MAN 3 (COMET 73P)
PLINTERS APART

MET TRAVELS
WN TRAIL OF
DURING MULTIPLE
AROUND THE
ERING SUN

ED COMPOSITE

R SPACE TELESCOPE
-TRAILING
ORBIT)

2006

LION MILES
MILLION KM)
ARTH

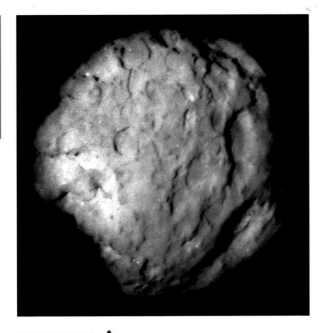

COMET WILD 2 (ABOVE)

CLOSE-UP VIEW
HIGHLIGHTS
SURFACE FEATURES

VISIBLE-LIGHT IMAGE

STARDUST SPACECRAFT

147 MILES (236KM)
FROM STARDUST

2 JANUARY 2004

242 MILLION MILES
(389 MILLION KM)
FROM EARTH

COMET TEMPEL 1 (OPPOSITE)

THIS IMAGE WAS COMPOSED
BY SCALING IMAGES
OBSERVED AT A DISTANCE
TO FIXED POINTS ON THE
COMET. THESE IMAGES WERE
REPLACED WITH IMAGES
ACQUIRED AT A CLOSER
RANGE ABOUT 4 SECONDS
BEFORE IMPACT.

VISIBLE-LIGHT COMPOSITE

DEEP IMPACT MISSION

A FEW METERS FROM
COMET SURFACE

4 JULY 2005 (IMPACT)

83 MILLION MILES
(133 MILLION KM)
FROM EARTH

New comets are usually named for their discoverers, such as Wild 2 after Swiss astronomer Paul Wild. Others, such as Halley, are named for those who calculated their orbits. Still others are named for the observatories or satellites involved in finding them.

On the eve of July Fourth 2005, NASA's Deep Impact space probe released an 800-pound (363kg), washing-machine-size impactor into the path of comet Tempel 1. Twenty-four hours later the impactor barreled into the comet, colliding in a fireworks display equivalent to detonating five tons of TNT. The blast from the crash jettisoned more than a thousand tons of Tempel 1 into space.

By analyzing clues from the encounter, research scientist Dr Carey M. Lisse of the John Hopkins Applied Physics Laboratory characterized the comet as an object about the size of a city "that has the strength of lemon meringue." It's fluffy, porous and about 75 percent empty space.

Clays, carbonates, silicates and only a small amount of water vapor were found in the ejected spray from Tempel 1. This proved contrary to the prevailing conception that comets are dirty snowballs made mostly of ice. What the impactor crashed into was more like a snowy dirtball — a frozen vault of dusty leftovers from our primordial solar system.

SATEL

LITES

HELD CAPTIVE BY GIANTS

SATELLITE

Just as the Sun is orbited by planets, so planets are orbited by moons. In our solar system, there are 140 known moons or natural satellites; 63 of them belong to Jupiter. All the other planets except Mercury and Venus have satellites, which vary in size from larger than Earth's Moon to small fragments of space rubble.

Some satellites may actually be asteroids that were caught by a planet's gravitational pull. Scientists speculate that Mars's Phobos and Deimos are asteroids. Saturn's Phoebe, several of Jupiter's satellites, and many of the moons of Uranus are also captured asteroids.

Although no satellites possess water as we know it, water ice exists on some, such as Europa and Ganymede. Beneath the icy surface of Europa and Enceladus, liquid oceans may even exist. Some moons have atmospheres; Saturn's Titan, for example, has a dense and hazy one.

Indeed, Titan's planetlike atmosphere serves as a kind of "prebiology lab," which may reveal things about Earth's own past. Other satellites, such as Jupiter's Europa, have very tenuous atmospheres. Europa's oxygen atmosphere is probably derived from water vapor, a product of the moon's icy landscape.

The Jovian satellite Io is the most volcanically active moon in our solar system. Volcanoes such as Io's Pele cover the moon's surface and continually renew the terrain with sulfurous ejections. The crust just below Io's surface is liquid because of the moon's extreme interior heat.

Then there are satellites with magnetic fields. Jupiter's Ganymede is the planet's largest moon and, indeed, the largest moon in the solar system. The particles from Ganymede's magnetic field rain down on the surface to produce a thin ozone layer.

SATURN'S ICY MOON DIONE

DIONE'S CRATERED TERRAIN AGAINST THE BACKDROP OF ITS HOST PLANET. SATURN'S RINGS ARE THE HORIZONTAL STRIPES ACROSS THE BOTTOM OF THE IMAGE.

VISIBLE-LIGHT AND INFRARED IMAGE (APPROXIMATE TRUE COLOR)

CASSINI ORBITER

24,000 MILES (39,000KM) FROM CASSINI

11 OCTOBER 2005

234,500 MILES (377,000KM) FROM DIONE TO SATURN

MOON

EARTH'S SATELLITE MOON
(LEFT)

DARK LAVA-FILLED MARIA
IN NORTHERN HEMISPHERE

NORTH POLAR MOSAIC OF
18 VISIBLE-LIGHT IMAGES

GALILEO ORBITER

564,000 MILES
(908,000KM)
FROM GALILEO

7 DECEMBER 1992

241,000 MILES
(389,000KM)
FROM EARTH

**EARTHRISE OBSERVED
FROM LUNAR ORBIT**
(RIGHT)

VISIBLE-LIGHT IMAGE

HANDHELD 70MM
HASSELBLAD THROUGH
MODULE WINDOW

APOLLO 17

DECEMBER 1972

239,000 MILES
(384,000KM)
APOLLO TO EARTH

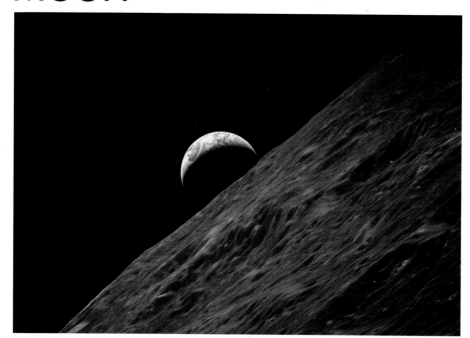

"MAGNIFICENT DESOLATENESS" IS how men who have walked on the Moon have described it. And although it is the only extraterrestrial body on which humans have landed, there is still so much we do not understand. It is a barren, cratered sphere, with no water or atmosphere, that orbits the Earth. Sometimes visible and sometimes vanished, it is always mysterious. The Moon is like a place that you cannot completely know, a place that always keeps some secrets.

Myth and mystery have surrounded our understanding of the Moon from ancient times.

According to superstition, a full Moon causes madness. The word lunatic comes from "luna," the Latin word for moon, and it literally means moonstruck. Europeans thought they saw the face of the "man in the moon," while Mayans believed they saw the face of a rabbit. Through the ages, the Moon has been a favorite subject for writers. In the 19th century, Jules Verne helped popularize science fiction when he wrote about space travel in stories such as FROM THE EARTH TO THE MOON.

Some of the allure may be due to the Moon's changing faces, or

phases. The Moon orbits Earth about once every month, and as it does, its apparent shape changes from a round ball, called a full Moon, to nothing at all, known as a new Moon.

Because the Moon does not produce its own light, we see only the half that is lit by the Sun. And we always see the same side of the Moon, the near side, because it is in synchronous rotation with the Earth. This means that it takes the same amount of time for the Moon to rotate on its own axis as it does to revolve around the Earth, 27.3 days.

Scientists are not sure how the Moon was formed. Many believe that it was created when an asteroid or small planetary body collided with Earth four-and-a-half billion years ago. That collision threw debris into orbit, which eventually joined together to become the Moon.

The Moon was hot and molten in the beginning. Over time, it cooled and formed a cratered outer layer, or mantle, and an iron core. There are two basic types of terrain on the Moon's near side: light, cratered high-lands called terrae (Latin for lands) surround darker, smoother maria (meaning seas, because early astronomers believed they were bodies of water). The craters were probably caused by the impact of meteorites on the Moon's surface; the largest are known as walled plains.

The moon has no atmosphere, and its gravity is weak — about one-sixth of Earth's. This means that a person who weighs 180 pounds (82kg) on Earth would weigh only 30 pounds (14kg) on the Moon. This proved to be a big help to the astronauts who went to the Moon because their space-suits, equipped with life-support systems, were very heavy. On 20 July 1969 — only 66 years after the Wright Brothers first flew — the American spacecraft Apollo 11 landed on the Sea of Tran-quillity, and Neil Armstrong became the first person to set foot on the Moon.

MOON: ORIENTAL BASIN

THE ORIENTAL BASIN, OR MARE Orientale, is viewed from Earth on the eastern rim of the Moon, at the boundary of its near and far sides. It is observable face on only from a spacecraft.

The saucer-shaped depres-sion, formed more than three billion years ago by an asteroid, measures 600 miles (1,000km) across. It consists of a shallow basin surrounded by three concentric rings of mountains, giving it the appearance of a bull's-eye. Like some 40 other craters on the Moon, this spec-tacular impact basin is called a mare, because it was thought to be an ocean. There is, of course, no water on the Moon.

Maria cover about 30 percent of the Moon's surface. Most are dark, flat regions that show evi-dence of past volcanic lava flow. Mare Orientale, the youngest of the Moon's impact basins, is not dark because it never filled with lava. Its basalt crust is also much shallower than those of Earth-facing mare, probably less than a mile deep.

**THE MARE ORIENTALE
IMPACT BASIN STRADDLES
THE NEAR AND FAR SIDES
OF THE MOON**

VISIBLE-LIGHT MOSAIC

LUNAR ORBITER 4

1,700 MILES (2,700KM)
FROM ORBITER

25 MAY 1967

239,000 MILES (384,000KM)
FROM EARTH

APOLLO 17: THE LAST MISSION

"ABSOLUTELY INCREDIBLE — YOU can see the boulder tracks — there are boulders all over," said Harrison Schmitt, the only geologist ever to explore the Moon.

The flight of Apollo 17 marked the end of an era. It was the last mission to land men on the Moon in the 20th century, and it is considered by many to be the capstone of NASA's Project Apollo.

In December 1972, the crew landed in the Taurus-Littrow region, a valley on the rim of the Sea of Serenity, and surveyed the geology of the landscape. The landing site was selected because it offered young volcanic rock as well as older mountainous wall material. The astronauts returned with the richest collection of rock and soil samples of any Apollo mission, 243 pounds (110kg).

Apollo 17 is memorable for other reasons. The astronauts remained on the lunar surface for 75 hours and covered more distance in the Lunar Rover Vehicle (or LRV, a four-wheeled manually controlled electric cart) than any other astronauts — 22 miles (35km). They also took 2,218 photographs, many of them shot sequentially for panoramic views. Schmitt and Mission Commander Eugene Cernan hold the distinction of being the last humans to walk on the lunar surface.

EUGENE CERNAN AND HARRISON SCHMITT EXPLORE THE TAURUS-LITTROW VALLEY, SEA OF SERENITY

VISIBLE-LIGHT IMAGES

70MM HASSELBLADS ATTACHED TO THE ASTRONAUTS' PRESSURE SUITS AT CHEST HEIGHT

APOLLO 17

DECEMBER 1972

239,000 MILES (384,000KM) FROM EARTH

Schmitt (shadow at left) photographs Cernan removing tools from the LRV. At far left is the Apollo Lunar Surface Experiments Package.
(120.48.56 HOURS INTO MISSION)

Geologist Schmitt uses a custom-made stainless steel rake to collect rock and soil samples.
(122.26.17 HOURS INTO MISSION)

An ancient boulder, thrown here by the impact that created the Sea of Serenity, is named Tracy's Rock, for Cernan's daughter.
(165.00.58 HOURS INTO MISSION)

PHOBOS

THE MOON PHOBOS WAS NAMED for a son of Mars, the Roman god of war. Phobos is the larger of Mars's two moons; the other is Deimos. Phobos measures 17 by 12 miles (28 by 20 km), and it circles the planet three times a Martian day.

The moon's most distinctive feature is Stickney, a six-mile-wide (10km) crater that was first identified in pictures from the Mariner 9 mission and later from the Viking 1 orbiter. Stickney was named after Chloe Angeline Stickney Hall, the wife of Asaph Hall, the astronomer who discovered both Phobos and Deimos in August 1877. The massive impact that formed the crater nearly destroyed Phobos and created streak patterns across the surface.

Phobos has no atmosphere, and its surface seems to consist of powder created by the constant bombardment of meteorites. The moon is composed of a carbon-rich rock similar to that found in certain asteroids.

The atmosphereless Phobos rapidly loses heat after sunset. As a result, the moon exhibits extremes in temperature from its day and night sides. Temperatures range from a high of about 25°F (−4°C) to a low of −170°F (−112°C).

The satellite's end is predictable. It will crash into Mars or break up in a ring. Approaching Mars at a rate of six feet (1.8m) every hundred years, Phobos is expected to collide with its planet in approximately 50 million years.

MARS'S SATELLITE PHOBOS WITH THE CRATER STICKNEY

VISIBLE-LIGHT COMPOSITE

VIKING 1 ORBITER

988 MILES (1,590KM) FROM VIKING

10 JUNE 1977

5,900 MILES (9,500KM) FROM PHOBOS TO MARS

IO

According to myth, Io was a young woman changed into a cow by Zeus to protect her from his wife's jealous rage. It didn't work. Hera recognized the girl and sent a gadfly to torment her. Io was left wandering throughout the Mediterranean. The satellite Io has been described as tormented too — but as a result of ongoing volcanic activity. Spewing from Io's violent vents, toxic concoctions, primarily of sulfur, continually spray paint the surface red, yellow and white.

Io is Jupiter's third largest moon and a little larger than our own. It is situated closest to Jupiter and is the innermost of the planet's four Galilean moons. Io has an iron core that takes up half its diameter, which means it could possibly have its own magnetic field. Auroras have been documented on Io by the Cassini spacecraft, resulting from an electric current running between the moon and Jupiter.

Io is the most volcanically active body in our solar system. The crust of the satellite is being constantly flexed due to the gravitational interplay between Jupiter and the moons Europa and Ganymede. For every four times Io goes around Jupiter, Europa goes around twice and Ganymede once. This phenomenon, known as orbital resonance, forces the normally circular orbits of these moons to follow more oblong paths. Because the distance between the satellites and Jupiter is constantly changing, the force of gravity on Io increases and decreases.

Just as a rubber ball can be heated by repeated squeezing and releasing, Io is heated by such gravitational flexing. This keeps the subsurface hot and drives Io's volcanic activity.

JUPITER'S SATELLITE IO

ASTRONOMERS NICKNAMED IO THE "PIZZA MOON" AFTER ITS WHITE, YELLOW, RED AND BLACK COLORATION. THE DIFFERENT COLORS REPRESENT SULFUR OR SULFUR COMPOUNDS FORMED AT DIFFERENT TEMPERATURES.

VISIBLE-LIGHT IMAGE (COLOR ENHANCED)

GALILEO ORBITER

310,000 MILES (500,000KM) FROM GALILEO

19 SEPTEMBER 1997

263,000 MILES (424,000KM) FROM IO TO JUPITER

IO: PELE ERUPTING

MOST OF IO'S VOLCANOES, LIKE Pele, are saucer-shaped, lacking the high peaks of shield volcanoes such as Mauna Loa and Mauna Kea on Earth. Classified as "paterae" (from the Latin for shallow dish), more than 400 scar Io's terrain, but only a few produce plumes.

Pele's umbrella-shaped dust plume can arch to a few hundred miles, but its giant form is faint against the surface and is easiest to see against the dark backdrop of interplanetary space. The source of Pele's dust plume appears to be a churning underground lava lake that regularly reveals its hot contents and raises sulfur-rich gases from Io's interior.

Most dust plumes are smaller and denser than Pele's. The smaller variety appear blue in daylight, contrasting with the warm hues of Io's landscape. Frosts deposited on the surface by these smaller plumes are thought to be responsible for resurfacing much of the moon.

PELE VOLCANO

A PLUME (UPPER RIGHT) IS EJECTED 186 MILES (300KM) ABOVE IO'S SURFACE

VISIBLE-LIGHT IMAGE (COLOR ENHANCED)

VOYAGER 1

331,000 MILES (532,000 MILLION KM) FROM VOYAGER 1

5 MARCH 1979

IO: THE BOND WITH JUPITER

AMONG ALL THE JOVIAN MOONS, Io has the strongest link with its mother planet. It's a complex relationship formed by Io's volcanic gases and Jupiter's powerful magnetic field. The bond takes shape as a halo.

Here's how it works. Neutral atoms of oxygen and sulfur gases are thrown into space by Io's volcanoes. The atoms become ionized by the Sun or by Jupiter's radiation belt. The ions (charged particles) around Io stick to invisible lines of intensity in Jupiter's magnetic field. The magnetic field moves in synchronization with Jupiter's rotation. As the magnetic field sweeps by Io, it drags with it ionized gas in circular paths, forming a dough-nut-shaped halo called a torus around the planet. What begins as a sphere of charged particles encompassing Io is molded into a halo surrounding Jupiter.

Wherever the torus passes through Jupiter's shadow, the faint glow becomes visible.

Meanwhile, as Io orbits Jupiter ensconced in the plan-et's torus, an intense stream of electrons flows along the planet's magnetic field lines, connecting Io to Jupiter at any given moment. Known as the Io flux tube, this electrical connec-tion between the two bodies travels around the planet with Io, instead of with Jupiter's much faster magnetic field. The flux tube permits periodic radio transmissions from a naturally generated Jovian source and is considered to be the largest electric circuit in the solar system.

THE SATELLITE IO IN ORBIT AROUND JUPITER

VISIBLE-LIGHT IMAGE

CASSINI ORBITER

6.2 MILLION MILES (9.9 MILLION KM) FROM CASSINI TO JUPITER

1 JANUARY 2001

262,000 MILES (422,000KM) FROM IO TO JUPITER

EUROPA

In Greek mythology, Europa was a beautiful princess seduced by Zeus, who was disguised as a white bull. The alluring surface of Europa, one of Jupiter's four Galilean moons, is unlike any other in the solar system. It is smooth and beautifully strange, with markings that resemble paint splashed across a palette.

The appearance may have been caused by water, since Europa is largely a ball of it. Some scientists believe that the markings result from global expansion. The moon's crust fractured. The cracks filled with water and froze.

Liquid water may also exist in Europa's interior. This might be a result of tidal heating initiated by gravitational influences. There is a constant tug of war, in which Jupiter is pulling on one side of the moon while the planet's other major moons are pulling on Europa's other side.

It is possible that Europa may have more water than Earth because it possesses a very deep mantle of water. Scientists believe that this water has a high salt content. Europa may have oceans as deep as 31 miles (50km) below its thin crust, which is at least three miles (5km) thick and is composed of water and ice.

Despite the tantalizing presence of water, Europa has only a fragile oxygen atmosphere. Sunlight and charged particles hit the icy surface and produce water vapor. Oxygen is released, but not enough to sustain life.

JUPITER'S SATELLITE EUROPA

CRACKS AND RIDGES ON THE FROZEN SURFACE

COMPOSITE IMAGE THROUGH GREEN, VIOLET AND NEAR-INFRARED FILTERS (COLOR ENHANCED)

GALILEO ORBITER

1,300 MILES (2,100KM) FROM GALILEO

1996–1998

417,000 MILES (671,000KM) FROM EUROPA TO JUPITER

TYPICAL LINEAR DOUBLE RIDGES ON EUROPA SUGGEST MOLTEN WATER ERUPTIONS

VISIBLE-LIGHT MOSAIC (COLOR ENHANCED)

GALILEO ORBITER

15,000 MILES (25,000KM) FROM GALILEO

28 JUNE 1996, 31 MAY 1998

417,000 MILES (671,000KM) FROM EUROPA TO JUPITER

GANYMEDE'S STAIR-STEP CLIFFS MAY HAVE BEEN FORMED BY TECTONIC FAULTING

VISIBLE-LIGHT IMAGE

GALILEO ORBITER

1,200 MILES (2,100KM) FROM GALILEO

20 MAY 2000

665,000 MILES (1,100,000KM) FROM GANYMEDE TO JUPITER

GANYMEDE

THE LARGEST OF JUPITER'S MOONS, Ganymede is the largest satellite in our solar system. If Jupiter can be compared to the hub of a great city, then Ganymede is the biggest building on the block. In fact, if Ganymede orbited the Sun, its size, basic composition of rock and ice and magnetic field would probably qualify it as a planet. It is 3,270 miles (5,262km) wide, larger than the planet Mercury.

Named for the youth who was cupbearer to the Olympian gods, Ganymede is made of a mostly rocky core, a water and ice mantle, and a crust of rock and ice. The satellite has what is considered a complex geological history, with mountains, valleys, craters and lava flow.

Ganymede's marbleized surface is covered by dark and light regions. The dark regions are heavily cratered, suggesting that they are extremely old. The brighter regions are believed to have been formed more recently, possibly by tectonic tension (the shifting of plates that compose the surface). These light regions have ridges and grooves that create a complex pattern, with formations that range from a few hundred to thousands of miles.

Although Ganymede has no substantial atmosphere, the Hubble Space Telescope detected a small amount of surface ozone. Scientists suspect that the ozone is produced by charged particles in Jupiter's magnetic field that rain down and mix with the icy surface, causing water in the ice to begin ozone production. The ozone suggests that Ganymede may have a thin and fragile oxygen atmosphere similar to that of its sister satellite Europa.

JUPITER'S SATELLITE GANYMEDE

VISIBLE-LIGHT MOSAIC (COLOR ENHANCED)

VOYAGER 2

186,000 MILES (300,000KM) FROM VOYAGER 2

26 JUNE 1996

665,000 MILES (1,100,000KM) TO JUPITER

MIMAS

MIMAS IS ONE OF THE INNERMOST satellites of Saturn. Like most of the planet's exotic moons, Mimas has a low density; it probably consists mostly of ice surrounding a small rocky core.

Mimas is unique for its colossal impact crater, 80 miles (130km) across, about a third of the moon's own diameter of 240 miles (400km) across. It gives the moon a superficial resemblance to the DEATH STAR battle station in the original STAR WARS film. The crater's steep walls are approximately three miles high (five km). The stalagmite-like central peak rises four miles (six km) above the crater floor, about the height of Mount Everest. The crater is named Herschel after the British astronomer William Herschel, who discovered Mimas in 1789.

This immense bull's-eye scar was made by a comet or asteroid that slammed into the moon long ago, almost destroying it. The collision was so titanic that fracture marks stretch all the way around to the opposite side of Mimas. The rest of the moon's surface is saturated with craters. This is evidence that Mimas, a frozen ball of ice bombarded by space debris billions of years ago, has remained essentially unchanged since then.

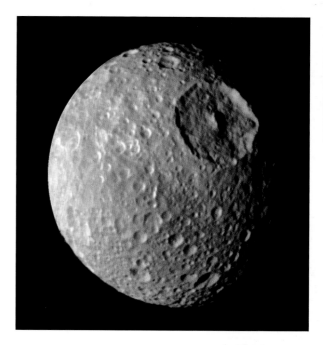

CRATER-LITTERED MIMAS AGAINST THE EXPANSE OF SATURN'S RINGS (OPPOSITE)

THE SMALLEST FEATURES SEEN ON THE MOON ARE APPROXIMATELY 440 YARDS (400M) ACROSS

VISIBLE-LIGHT IMAGE

CASSINI ORBITER

42,000 MILES (68,000KM) FROM CASSINI

2 AUGUST 2005

116,500 MILES (188,000KM) FROM MIMAS TO SATURN

MIMAS SHOWS OFF ITS MOST PROMINENT FEATURE, THE HERSCHEL CRATER (ABOVE)

VISIBLE-LIGHT IMAGE

CASSINI ORBITER

141,000 MILES (227,000KM) FROM CASSINI

1 AUGUST 2005

117,000 MILES (189,000KM) FROM MIMAS TO SATURN

ENCELADUS

THE BLUE "TIGER STRIPES" ARE THE FRACTURES THROUGH WHICH FINE ICE PARTICLES MAY SPOUT FROM A WATERY INTERIOR (LEFT)

MOSAIC IN FALSE-COLOR ULTRAVIOLET TO INFRARED WAVELENGTHS

CASSINI ORBITER

38,000–7,000 MILES (61,000–11,000 KM) FROM CASSINI

14 JULY 2005

148,000 MILES (238,000KM) FROM ENCELADUS TO SATURN

ENCELADUS BACKLIT BY THE SUN (ABOVE)

THE ICY JET SPRAY OFF THE LOWER LEFT IS BELIEVED TO BE GEYSERS ERUPTING FROM PRESSURIZED UNDERGROUND WATER

VISIBLE-LIGHT IMAGE

CASSINI ORBITER

92,000 MILES (148,000KM) FROM CASSINI

27 NOVEMBER 2005

148,500 MILES (239,000KM) FROM ENCELADUS TO SATURN

FIRST PHOTOGRAPHED BY THE Voyager 1 spacecraft in 1980, it was clear that Enceladus, the tenth moon from Saturn, was unusual. While parts of the satellite appear heavily cratered, others appear relatively smooth. A smooth surface suggests that geologic activity paved away the ancient craters.

Later images by the Cassini spacecraft reveal several different types of terrain, including the huge blue cracks slicing across the icy white surface of the south polar landscape. These so-called "tiger stripes" are a few hundred degrees warmer than the surrounding area – indicating that the interior of the moon may be liquid today.

Enceladus is the only Saturnian moon other than Titan known to have an atmosphere. This is puzzling because Enceladus, at a diameter of 310 miles (500km), is only one-seventh the diameter of Titan. This means the amount of gravity on the moon is not enough to hold an atmosphere for long. Therefore some process on the moon must be replenishing it.

The source of Enceladus's atmosphere was discovered in 2005 when the Cassini probe pictured fountainlike plumes of icy particles jetting out from the moon's south polar region. Unlike the magma volcanoes on Earth and Venus, these are called "cryovolcanoes" because they pump out water and ammonia rather than molten rock.

The amount of water pouring out of Enceladus at any given time is comparable to the eruption of the Old Faithful geyser in Yellowstone National Park in the U.S. Some of the water gets caught by the moon's gravity and is pulled back down, resulting in a pure white snowfall over an older rock-hard icy crust – like a snow-making machine at a ski resort. The white snow explains why Enceladus is one of the brightest objects in the solar system, reflecting essentially 100 percent of its sunlight.

Some of the water gets squirted out with such force that it escapes from the moon entirely and falls into orbit around Saturn, replenishing the mysterious E ring, the widest and most diffuse ring and the only one with a bluish tint.

Pockets of water, not far below Enceladus's surface, must feed the geysers. These hidden oceans would have to be substantial to have fueled the geysers for billions of years. What's more, the moon's interior must stay heated by the gravitational tug of war with Saturn and the neighboring moons. All these clues suggest that microbial life could perhaps survive in the underground water world of Enceladus.

TITAN

THE SECRETS OF TITAN, SATURN'S largest moon, have long been guarded by its dense atmosphere. But on 14 January 2005, the Huygens probe parachuted down through Titan's thick haze.

As it descended, Huygens transmitted data back to its mother ship, the Cassini orbiter, which had carried it on its seven-year journey to the Saturn system. Huygens (named for the Dutch astronomer Christiaan Huygens, who discovered Titan in 1655) captured images, sampled the atmosphere and reported climatic conditions. It made a soft landing on a sand-like area, bathed in light from Titan's distinctive orange sky. Its main mission accomplished, Huygens continued transmitting information for 72 minutes before Cassini disappeared below the horizon.

Named after the race of giant gods who ruled the heavens in Greek mythology, Titan was once thought to be the largest satellite in the solar system. At 3,200 miles (5,500km) in diameter, however, it is actually second in size to Jupiter's Ganymede, though it is still bigger than the planet Mercury. Titan circles Saturn every 16 days at a distance of about 750,000 miles (1.2 million km).

What makes Titan unique is that it is the only moon in the solar system known to have an atmosphere even denser than Earth's. It also has surface features that bear a striking resemblance to Earth. River channels appear carved into the landscape, flowing into lake beds, complete with shoals. It is evidence of a process much like the one that shaped Earth's surface – but the chemistry is dramatically different.

Water on the satellite remains permanently frozen because of frigid –275°F (–170°C) temperatures, and the "rocks" that litter the landscape are in fact frozen water ice. But methane (the odorless, colorless gas that is the main component of natural gas) can exist as either liquid or gas due to the extreme cold and intense atmospheric pressure. It is methane vapor that rises from the moon's chilly surface to warm, liquefy and fall as rain in Titan's nitrogen atmosphere.

Because methane in Titan's atmosphere is destroyed by sunlight, producing hydrocarbons responsible for the moon's thick layer of haze, there must be a surface source that continually replenishes it. Along with nitrogen and ethane, Huygens detected traces of argon 40, which is evidence of volcanic activity. What the volcanoes of Titan have spewed, however, is not lava but water ice and ammonia.

TITAN'S ATMOSPHERIC SHROUD (ABOVE)

COMPOSITE OF 4 ULTRAVIOLET AND INFRARED IMAGES (COLOR ADDED)

CASSINI ORBITER

746 MILES (1,200KM) FROM CASSINI

26 OCTOBER 2004

780,000 MILES (1.3 MILLION KM) FROM TITAN TO SATURN

AERIAL VIEW OF TITAN EXTENDING TO 40 MILES (64KM)

COMPOSITE OF 30 NEAR-INFRARED IMAGES

HUYGENS PROBE

5–8 MILES (8–13KM) FROM HUYGENS

14 JANUARY 2005

750,000 MILES (1.2 MILLION KM) FROM TITAN TO SATURN

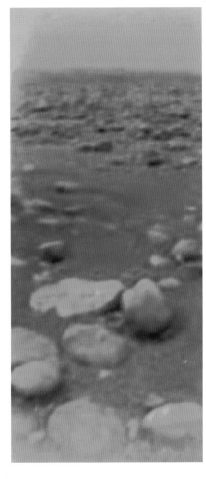

**ROCKS OF FROZEN
WATER REST ON A MIX OF
HYDROCARBON AND
WATER-ICE SEDIMENTS**
(LEFT)

NEAR-INFRARED IMAGE
(APPROXIMATE TRUE COLOR)

HUYGENS PROBE

THE TWO ROCKLIKE OBJECTS
JUST BELOW CENTER ARE
33 INCHES (85CM) FROM THE
HUYGENS PROBE

14 JANUARY 2005

**AERIAL VIEWS OF TITAN
AROUND THE HUYGENS
LANDING SITE AS FLATTENED
MERCATOR PROJECTIONS**
(ABOVE)

NEAR-INFRARED IMAGES
(APPROXIMATE TRUE COLOR)

HUYGENS PROBE

100–0.25 MILES
(150–0.4KM) FROM TITAN

14 JANUARY 2005

750,000 MILES
(1.2 MILLION KM)
FROM TITAN TO SATURN

**EVIDENCE OF LIQUID
LAKES ON TITAN**
(RIGHT)

THE BLUE LAKES ARE
DARKER THAN
THE SURROUNDING
TAN TERRAIN

RADAR IMAGE
(COLOR ADDED)

CASSINI ORBITER

590 MILES
(950KM)
FROM CASSINI

22 JULY 2006

780,000 MILES
(1.3 MILLION KM)
FROM TITAN TO SATURN

HYPERION

Saturn's Hyperion has the distinction of being the largest irregularly shaped moon ever observed. It is not spherical but shaped more like a hockey puck. About every 64 days, Hyperion encounters Titan, its giant satellite neighbor. Titan's gravitational tug on nonspherical Hyperion causes its normally stable spin to go haywire, changing both its rotation rate and its axis.

Composed largely of water ice with only a small amount of rock, Hyperion's bizarre sponge-like appearance is due to the deep, sharp-edged craters peppering the surface.

Close in color to the dark Saturnian moon Iapetus, Hyperion's reddish hue suggests that the two bodies have a kinship. Hyperion may be a fragment of a larger body broken up by a comet collision. This may have injected material into space, causing one side of Iapetus, the once snow-white neighboring moon, to be coated with dark dust.

POCK-MARKED HYPERION (MAIN IMAGE)

THE MOON'S RED COLOR WAS TONED DOWN AND OTHER COLORS ENHANCED TO MAKE SURFACE VARIATIONS MORE APPARENT

VISIBLE-LIGHT IMAGE

CASSINI ORBITER

38,500 MILES (62,000KM) FROM CASSINI

26 SEPTEMBER 2005

HYPERION'S ODDBALL ORBIT IS CAUSED BY FREQUENT INTERACTION WITH TITAN (FAR RIGHT)

VISIBLE-LIGHT IMAGES

CASSINI ORBITER

900,000 MILES (1.45 MILLION KM) FROM CASSINI

OCTOBER 2004, FEBRUARY 2005

920,000 MILES (1.5 MILLION KM) FROM HYPERION TO SATURN

PHOEBE

ACCORDING TO DATA SENT BACK from the Cassini spacecraft, Saturn's moon Phoebe is probably a frozen remnant from the formation of the solar system more than four billion years ago.

Readings from the Cassini Orbiter confirm that Phoebe is composed of a primordial mixture of ice, rock and carbon. Surprisingly, Phoebe's composition seems to be more like that of a comet than a typical rocky moon.

What distinguishes Phoebe is its orbit. About 132 miles (212km) wide, the satellite turns on its axis every nine hours and takes roughly 18 months to complete a revolution around Saturn. But it orbits Saturn in retrograde, the opposite direction of most other moons and objects in the solar system. It also orbits far away from Saturn – eight million miles (13 million km).

Unlike most Saturnian moons, Phoebe reflects very little sunlight. Phoebe's darkness and its retrograde orbit have led scientists to speculate that it is a captured object (one that is trapped by the gravity of a bigger body, usually a planet).

Scientists believe that Phoebe and bodies like it were abundant in the outer reaches of the solar system. They formed the building blocks of that part called the Kuiper Belt, a ring-shaped area extending from Neptune outward. Phoebe apparently moved to the inner solar system and then became trapped in Saturn's orbit.

SATURN'S SATELLITE PHOEBE

MOSAIC OF 6 VISIBLE-LIGHT IMAGES

CASSINI ORBITER

7,700 MILES (12,400KM) FROM CASSINI

11 JUNE 2004

8 MILLION MILES (13 MILLION KM) FROM PHOEBE TO SATURN

TRITON

Discovered barely a month after Neptune, Triton is named for the son of Poseidon, Greek god of the sea. Neptune's largest moon, Triton is the coldest object in our solar system. Its surface temperature is −390°F (−235°C). If you had to find a comparison here on Earth — and there really isn't one — imagine Antarctica in the dead of winter.

Triton has a weak atmosphere composed of clouds of nitrogen ice particles. In fact, the satellite is one of only three objects to possess large amounts of nitrogen in its atmosphere. (The others are Earth and Titan, Saturn's largest satellite.) Triton is relatively dense and is made up of more rock than the icy moons of Saturn and Uranus.

What makes Triton unusual is its rotation. Like Saturn's Phoebe, Triton orbits its planet in retrograde — meaning that it is circling opposite to Neptune's rotation. Scientists speculate that Triton may be a captured object because of its retrograde orbit and high density. They believe that Neptune might have pulled it into its orbit as the planet traveled through space several billion years ago.

Triton's surface is relatively young, as suggested by the scarcity of visible craters. There are also large cracks. In addition, active geysers of nitrogen gas and dark dust have been observed erupting from the surface. The Voyager 2 spacecraft recorded plumes up to several miles high.

Because of Triton's frigid temperatures, most of the atmosphere's nitrogen freezes. That makes Triton the only moon in the solar system with a surface composed of nitrogen ice. This, along with methane ice, creates the colorful streaks in Triton's southern polar cap.

NEPTUNE'S SATELLITE TRITON

COMPOSITE IMAGE THROUGH GREEN, VIOLET AND ULTRAVIOLET FILTERS

VOYAGER 2

330,000 MILES (530,000KM) FROM VOYAGER 2

24 AUGUST 1989

221,000 MILES (355,000KM) FROM TRITON TO NEPTUNE

GALA

AXIES

STAR
ATTRACTION

GALAXY

A GALAXY IS A GIGANTIC GROUPING of stars, a kind of metropolis. Like all cities, galaxies evolve over time. They are fluid structures in a constant state of change.

Gravity pulls together the dark and luminous matter that fills interstellar space to create galaxies. Gravity holds them together and also brings them together. They collide and merge, which is usually how galaxies grow. And it is because of gravity that galaxies congregate in galactic clusters. The Milky Way is just one of about three dozen galaxies in a cluster known as the Local Group.

Galaxies come in a huge assortment of sizes. Jumbo galaxies can have as many as 3,000 billion stars, as well as other stars-in-the-making. Even the smallest galaxies are likely to have approximately 200,000 stars. Our own galaxy, the Milky Way, holds between 100 billion and 200 billion.

There are three basic galactic forms. Elliptical galaxies are shaped more or less like oval balls. They are also the largest.

Spiral galaxies, such as our own Milky Way, typically have a bulging center and slender, curving arms in a disk. Irregular galaxies, which have no defined shape, are usually small and have relatively few stars.

In his classification of galaxies, Edwin Hubble said that spirals evolved from ellipticals. Scientists now believe that it is the other way around: Spirals merged to form ellipticals.

**SOMBRERO GALAXY (M 104)
IN THE VIRGO CLUSTER**

NEARLY EDGE-ON VIEW,
50,000 LIGHT-YEARS ACROSS

VISIBLE-LIGHT MOSAIC

HUBBLE SPACE TELESCOPE
(EARTH-ORBITING)

MAY–JUNE 2003

28 MILLION LIGHT-YEARS
FROM EARTH

DWARF GALAXY

THE BEST MODEL FOR THE BIRTH of galaxies in the early universe predicts an invisible form of matter known only by its gravitational force. Because this matter is missing light, it is called dark matter. Not long after the Big Bang, dark matter was able to attract ordinary matter in the form of vast clouds of gas. The thickest clouds contracted to form stars and galaxies. Dwarf galaxies were the first to emerge.

Because the newborn galaxies were small, gravity was low. Matter could escape and merge with other matter, seeding the universe with dwarf galaxies. These then grew by clumping together to form larger galaxies, or were digested by large galaxies that grew by cannibalizing small ones. Modern galactic structures such as spirals and ellipticals descended from these diminutive forebears.

Dwarf galaxies are typically irregular in shape, some more spherical than others. It is thought that the earliest dwarf was a flat disk. As the primordial disk continually merged with other infant galaxies, the flat structure of stars was tossed around, becoming more spheroidal. Both varieties are still common today. The Milky Way has about a dozen dwarf satellite galaxies. These survivors did not get caught up in typical galactic mergers. One of the satellites, Sagittarius Dwarf Irregular (right), is spheroidal. It is dim and spread out because it is slowly being stretched apart by the Milky Way's irresistible gravity.

SAGITTARIUS DWARF IRREGULAR GALAXY (SAGDIG)

THE FAINT CONGLOMERATION OF STARS IS A SATELLITE GALAXY OF THE MILKY WAY

VISIBLE-LIGHT IMAGE

HUBBLE SPACE TELESCOPE (EARTH-ORBITING)

18 AUGUST 2003

3.5 MILLION LIGHT-YEARS FROM EARTH

SPIRAL GALAXY

Spiral galaxies are the most ubiquitous cities of stars in the universe. They are broad, flattened disks of stars, dust and gas, distinguished by long, curving, blue-white arms that wind around a bright central bulge of older stars. Until a century ago, they were thought of as "spiral nebulas" around nearby newborn stars. But they were simply too far away for individual stars to be resolved without a large telescope.

Within these starry pancakes there is an ongoing "galactic ecology" where stellar debris is recycled into successive generations of stars. Galactic disks would be largely indistinguishable from each other were it not for density waves (analogous to ripples on a pond). The wave action is thought to create the spiral arms, where gas and dust pile up and ignite into firestorms of star birth.

Computer simulations show that the arms are dynamic and can re-form in other regions of the disk. If the arms did not change, over time they would wind up tightly, like a watch spring, as the galaxy rotates. But they do not. This complex and not fully understood process makes each spiral galaxy as unique as individual snowflakes.

Spiral galaxies were created from the merger of smaller galaxies in the early universe. By the time the universe was half its present age, the spirals were fully formed. But the evolution has not ended. When spiral galaxies merge, they create elliptical galaxies as the stars are scattered out of the plane of the disks. In our galactic neighborhood, the Milky Way is the second largest spiral after the Andromeda Galaxy, 2.5 million light-years away. The two spirals are speeding toward each other at 300,000 miles (483,000km) per hour. In several billion years they may collide and form one enormous elliptical galaxy.

FACE-ON VIEW OF A DUSTY SPIRAL GALAXY (NGC 3370) IN THE CONSTELLATION LEO

VISIBLE-LIGHT IMAGE

HUBBLE SPACE TELESCOPE (EARTH-ORBITING)

APRIL–MAY 2003

98 MILLION LIGHT-YEARS FROM EARTH

WHIRLPOOL GALAXY

M 51 IS A CLASSIC SPIRAL
GALAXY, FROM ITS CURVING
ARMS, WHERE NEWBORN
STARS RESIDE, TO ITS
YELLOWISH CENTER, HOME
TO OLDER STARS

VISIBLE-LIGHT IMAGE

HUBBLE SPACE TELESCOPE
(EARTH-ORBITING)

18—22 JANUARY 2005

31 MILLION LIGHT-YEARS
FROM EARTH

BARRED SPIRAL GALAXY

A PROMINENT BARLIKE FEATURE IS thought to appear in roughly one-third of spiral galaxies. In fact, recent observations indicate that the Milky Way has a longer bar than previously thought. This galactic type is identified by the presence of stars and inter-stellar matter along a bar in the central bulge, with spiral arms swirling from the ends.

One current theory is that most barred spirals result from interactions with nearby galax-ies, which set up instabilities in the spiral disk. The encounter gravitationally rearranges the rotation of some stars from circular orbits to more elliptical ones. These stars trace out the barlike pattern. They also rob momentum from gas in the disk so that it flows toward the center of the galaxy along the bar. Shock waves prevent clouds from collapsing and forming new stars in the bar.

In the case of the Milky Way, scientists were able to determine the size of the bar by measuring the velocities of hydrogen, which respond to the gravity of the stars, and by measuring starlight in infrared, which sees through interstellar pollution.

A galaxy with a smaller bar is the barred spiral galaxy NGC 7424, at left. This galaxy, at about 100,000 light-years across, is in the intermediate class of galaxies between nor-mal spirals and those that are strongly barred. Surrounding the radiant golden bar of NGC 7424 are bluish-gray winding arms, studded with red dots. The bluish hues indicate the pres-ence of massive young stars and the reddish dots signify areas of star formation.

**THE BARRED SPIRAL
GALAXY NGC 7424 IN THE
CONSTELLATION GRUS**
(LEFT)

VISIBLE-LIGHT COMPOSITE

EUROPEAN SOUTHERN
OBSERVATORY
VIMOS + 8.2M VLT
MELIPAL TELESCOPE

9 OCTOBER 2004

40 MILLION LIGHT-YEARS
FROM EARTH

ELLIPTICAL GALAXY

AS AGEING SPIRAL GALAXIES engulf and devour each other, the injured disks lose their shape, scattering the orbits of stars, almost like a swarm of bees. The newly configured structure swells into a star-studded sphere known as an elliptical galaxy.

Ellipticals are like gigantic cotton balls in the sky. Their 3-D shape can range from nearly round to oval. Since they do not have enough dust or gas to sustain star formation, ellipticals are usually yellow-red in color due to their older star population, compared with the blue cast of spirals with younger stars. Elliptical galaxies are common among large, crowded galaxy clusters, supporting the theory that they form through mergers and collisions.

NGC 1316 in the constellation Fornax (right) looks like a typical elliptical galaxy, but it is caught in the act of swallowing a smaller disk galaxy. Traces of spiral arms and a disk are evidence that the fusion is not yet complete.

THE GIANT ELLIPTICAL GALAXY NGC 1316 IN THE CONSTELLATION FORNAX

VEINED DUST LANES SHOW THAT NGC 1316 IS MERGING WITH A SPIRAL GALAXY

VISIBLE-LIGHT IMAGE

HUBBLE SPACE TELESCOPE (EARTH-ORBITING)

4, 7 MARCH 2003

75 MILLION LIGHT-YEARS FROM EARTH

IRREGULAR GALAXY

An irregular galaxy is what it sounds like – disorganized. It does not have a distinct spiral or elliptical shape. Irregular galaxies are grouped by their independent nature because they don't fit anywhere else.

Sometimes irregulars exist in isolation and sometimes they are formed by collisions, near misses and gravitational forces as they interact with other galaxies. Irregulars are smaller than spiral or elliptical galaxies. Most are low-mass galaxies composed of millions, not billions, of stars.

From the Southern Hemisphere, two prime irregular galaxies can be spotted with the unaided eye – the Large and Small Magellanic Clouds. These two satellite galaxies are gravitationally bound to the Milky Way and are being stretched by the attraction of the larger galaxy.

The irregular dwarf galaxy here is located in the constellation Sagittarius in the Milky Way's Local Group. With a heavy population of hot, massive blue stars, Barnard's Galaxy is located in our neighborhood, just 1.6 million light-years away. The gas bubble at the one o'clock position is a cocoon of stars born in the gas cloud. Spirited stellar winds from the baby stars pushed the extra gas from the cloud into space, where it expands without interference or interruption.

BARNARD'S GALAXY (NGC 6822), A DWARF IRREGULAR GALAXY IN THE CONSTELLATION SAGITTARIUS

VISIBLE-LIGHT IMAGE (REPRESENTATIVE COLOR)

NSF BLANCO 4M TELESCOPE AT CERRO TOLOLO INTER-AMERICAN OBSERVATORY, NOAO

1, 2 SEPTEMBER 2000

1.6 MILLION LIGHT-YEARS FROM EARTH

SEYFERT GALAXY

A Seyfert galaxy is a special spiral galaxy with an energetic center. This compact and active core, or nucleus, releases bright clouds and filaments. Excited matter is propelled by a superwind created by a supermassive black hole. Seyfert galaxies are part of a class of objects called Active Galactic Nuclei (AGN). These have the ability to blow gas from their cores at high speed due to active central black holes.

In the photographs, the central fountainlike shape is a bubble of gas being blown by winds released in a burst of star formation. In the close-up above, four streams of gaseous filaments shoot above the disk at more than four million miles (six million km) an hour. The gas whirls around in a vortex and is expelled into space. Eventually, gas will rain down on the galaxy's disk, where it may collide with gas clouds, compress them and form new stars. Many astronomers think that all spirals erupt now and then. Our own Milky Way may once have been or will be a Seyfert galaxy.

**THE SEYFERT GALAXY
NGC 3079** (RIGHT)
**AND A CLOSE-UP OF
ITS CORE** (TOP)

VISIBLE-LIGHT IMAGE

HUBBLE SPACE TELESCOPE
(EARTH-ORBITING)

26 NOVEMBER 1998

50 MILLION LIGHT-YEARS
FROM EARTH

STARBURST GALAXY

A STARBURST GALAXY IS A BRIEF but vivid firestorm of star birth. For about 10 million years — a relatively short burst in the life of a 10-billion-year-old galaxy — star formation occurs at hundreds of times the rate it does in normal galaxies. The young stars are big and bright, so starbursts stand out as the most luminous galaxies in the sky.

The high birthrate is probably spawned by a close encounter or collision with another galaxy. Shock waves cause giant clouds of gas and dust to collapse and form stars. The young stars burn out quickly because they are so massive, and they explode as supernovas. A chain reaction of shock waves and star formation drives through the galactic center, where most of the gas is located. The burst of activity stops once most of the gas has been used up or blown away.

In our local universe, starburst galaxies are rare now, but they were more common billions of years ago. All galaxies were closer together then, so they were more likely to bump into one another. More frequent encounters produced more starbursts as galactic forms evolved with the expanding universe.

THE CIGAR GALAXY (M 82)

STARS ARE BEING BORN IN THE GALACTIC CENTER TEN TIMES FASTER THAN IN OUR MILKY WAY. THE SUPERWIND GENERATED BY THESE STARS COMPRESSES ENOUGH GAS TO MAKE MILLIONS MORE.

THIS COLOR-CODED COMPOSITE IS A COLLABORATION OF THREE NASA OBSERVATORIES

X-RAY IN BLUE,
INFRARED IN RED,
VISIBLE LIGHT IN ORANGE
AND YELLOW-GREEN

CHANDRA X-RAY OBSERVATORY
18 JUNE 2002

SPITZER SPACE TELESCOPE
(INFRARED), 6, 8, 9 MAY 2005

HUBBLE SPACE TELESCOPE
(VISIBLE LIGHT),
27–29 MARCH 2006

12 MILLION LIGHT-YEARS
FROM EARTH

WARPED GALAXY

A GALAXY LIKE THE MILKY WAY is basically a thin, flat disk, but its outer regions are slightly warped, almost like the brim of a hat, bending down on one side and up on the other. This warping is now known to be common in spiral galaxies.

Far more pronounced warping is shown in the gently undulating disk above, an edge-on view of galaxy ESO 510-G13 in the constellation Hydra.

The large spiral is in the process of digesting a smaller galaxy with which it has collided, causing distortion of the disk by gravitational forces. The twisted structure is illuminated by the central bulge. Eventually, after the merger settles down, the spiral galaxy will become more regular in appearance. ESO 510-G13 was first seen in photographs taken by the European Southern Observatory.

AN EDGE-ON VIEW OF THE WARPED GALAXY ESO 510-G13

THE TWISTED DISK STRUCTURE INDICATES A RECENT COLLISION WITH A NEARBY GALAXY

VISIBLE-LIGHT IMAGE

HUBBLE SPACE TELESCOPE (EARTH-ORBITING)

6–7 APRIL 2001

150 MILLION LIGHT-YEARS FROM EARTH

LENTICULAR GALAXY

WHEN VIEWED EDGE ON, LENTICU-lar galaxies are shaped like a double-convex lens. When viewed face on, they resemble elliptical galaxies, which are more spherical.

These unusual galaxies might seem to be a transitional stage between spirals and ellipticals. The rotund appearance, how-ever, probably has a different origin. Lenticulars could be spiral galaxies with the arms wound tight — so tight around the center that they have disap-peared into an accentuated bulge and bulbous shape.

In lenticular galaxy NGC 2787 (below), evidence of the vanishing arms is visible in the concentric rings of swirling dust around the bright nucleus.

THE LENTICULAR GALAXY NGC 2787
VISIBLE-LIGHT IMAGE
HUBBLE SPACE TELESCOPE (EARTH-ORBITING)
29 JANUARY 1999
24 MILLION LIGHT-YEARS FROM EARTH

BACKWARD SPIRAL GALAXY

A BACKWARD SPIRAL GETS ITS name from its outer arms of gas and stars, which lead in the direction of the galaxy's rotation. In most spirals, such as the Milky Way, these density lanes trail behind the direction of rotation, as if following in its wake. The backward spiral here also has a quirky inner arm, which is rotating in the opposite direction. The likely explanation is that NGC 4622 was disturbed by a smaller galaxy, which it is in the process of incorporating.

THE BACKWARD SPIRAL GALAXY NGC 4622
VISIBLE-LIGHT COMPOSITE
HUBBLE SPACE TELESCOPE (EARTH-ORBITING)
25 MAY 2001
111 MILLION LIGHT-YEARS FROM EARTH

GALACTIC CENTER

IN THE DIRECTION OF THE CON-stellation Sagittarius, about 25,000 light-years away from Earth, millions of stars are huddled together in the galactic center of the Milky Way.

The outermost region of the center, 500 light-years wide, is known as the bulge. In the large image, the bulge is visible at lower left, glowing behind a mottled foreground of dust. The strong point of light within the glow is the inner core — a dense mass of stars 30 light-years wide. The inner core can be seen in the close-up at right. Hidden in the clouds is a three-armed feature called the Mini-Spiral, which surrounds our central supermassive black hole.

This black hole, known as Sagittarius A* (pronounced A star), is the geometric center of our galaxy. It weighs in at three million times the mass of our Sun and its event horizon spans some 24 million miles (39 million km). Black holes at the center of galaxies have huge appetites. They binge on interstellar gas and dust and emit radiation. The emissions from Sagittarius A* are comparatively weak, suggesting that explosive events have cleared away its supply of gaseous food.

THE GALACTIC CENTER OF THE MILKY WAY GALAXY IN THE CONSTELLATION SAGITTARIUS
(LEFT)

THE BULGE IN THE REGION AT LOWER LEFT HARBORS THE BLACK HOLE

INFRARED COMPOSITE IMAGE REVEALS OTHERWISE HIDDEN STARS

2MASS
(EARTH-BASED)

APRIL 1997, MARCH 2001

25,000 LIGHT-YEARS FROM EARTH

THE SUPERMASSIVE BLACK HOLE SAGITTARIUS A* IS AT THE CORE OF THE MILKY WAY
(TOP)

X-RAY IMAGE

CHANDRA X-RAY OBSERVATORY
(EARTH-ORBITING)

21 SEPTEMBER 1999–4 JUNE 2002

25,000 LIGHT-YEARS FROM EARTH

GALACTIC PLANE

On a dark moonless night, sky-watchers can see a broad ribbon of starlight spanning horizon to horizon, like a giant seam on the sky. The Greeks imagined it was a river of milk from the goddess Hera. Today we know it as the Milky Way.

When we see the Milky Way, we are really looking along the plane of our galaxy. The galactic disk is 100,000 light-years in diameter and 3,000 light-years thick. This gives it the proportion of an old-fashioned LP phonograph record.

The plane is a large flattened disk of stars that is rich in interstellar gas and dust. The dust obscures bright stars as a dense fog hides the bright lights of a city skyline.

Our Sun and solar system lie about halfway between the center of the disk and its outer boundary. From this perspective, Spitzer's infrared telescope penetrates the cosmic haze to give us a peek deep into the galaxy's starry disk.

In this edge-on picture, old and cool stars are blue, while dust features warmed by blazing hot, massive stars are reddish. The red dust clouds have been illuminated by nearby star

formation, and indicate the presence of large organic molecules mixed in with the dust. The plane of the Milky Way's flat disk is apparent as the main horizontal band of clouds.

The patches of black are obscuring dust clouds that are so dense they block even infrared light from Spitzer's supersensitive gaze. Bright arcs of white throughout the image are star-forming regions.

PANORAMIC EDGE-ON VIEW OF THE MILKY WAY'S PLANE SPANNING A 9° SWATH OF GALACTIC REAL ESTATE

THIS IS AN ENTIRELY NEW SKELETAL VIEW OF OUR GALAXY IN MID-INFRARED. AT THIS WAVELENGTH GALACTIC ACTIVITY IS NOT BLOCKED BY THE FINE DUST THAT OBSCURES VISIBLE AND ULTRAVIOLET VIEWS.

GLIMPSE PROJECT
SPITZER SPACE TELESCOPE
(EARTH-TRAILING
SOLAR ORBIT)

31 MARCH–2 APRIL 2004

A FEW HUNDRED LIGHT-YEARS FROM EARTH TO TENS OF THOUSANDS OF LIGHT-YEARS AWAY

MERGERS

THE NEARBY UNIVERSE IS FULL of stately spiral and elliptical galaxies. They appear majestic and quiescent in large telescopes. Ever since Edwin Hubble discovered galaxies beyond the Milky Way in the early 1920s, astronomers have wondered how these galaxies formed. Were they born that way? Did they gravitationally collapse from a larger cloud of primordial hydrogen? Only in the past two decades have observations of the very distant early universe revealed a different and discordant universe from the one around us today.

The Hubble Space Telescope reveals that galaxies in the early universe experienced multiple and spectacular mergers. The small galaxy mergers billions of years ago are like many little brooks coming together to form streams, which then converge into a wide river. Ten billion years ago, nearly all galaxies were in the process of merging. Such mergers are very rare today. Only about 1 percent of galaxies are undergoing mergers in our local universe.

We do have some current examples of the cosmic "Clash of the Titans" that occurs when two massive spiral galaxies crash into each other. One of the most dramatic is the Mice (above). The long tails of young stars are the signature of the gravitational tidal pull between the two galaxies, which will eventually combine to form a gigantic sphere – an elliptical galaxy.

Views of nearby collisions provide insights into the Milky Way's own future. In about five billion years our galaxy will pro-

bably collide with Andromeda. At a distance of 2.5 million light-years, it is our nearest neighboring large galaxy. As is beginning with the Mice galaxies, the collision will destroy the stately pinwheel of stars and, over a billion years, Andromeda and the Milky Way will be transformed into one gigantic spherical galaxy.

THE MICE (NGC 4676 A AND B) IN THE CONSTELLATION COMA BERENICES (ABOVE)

THESE NEARLY IDENTICAL COLLIDING SPIRAL GALAXIES EVENTUALLY WILL MERGE INTO AN ELLIPTICAL GALAXY

VISIBLE-LIGHT IMAGE

HUBBLE SPACE TELESCOPE (EARTH ORBITING)

7 APRIL 2002

ABOUT 300 MILLION LIGHT-YEARS FROM EARTH

IC 2163 (RIGHT) **IS SWINGING PAST NGC 2207** (LEFT) **IN A COUNTERCLOCKWISE DIRECTION** (FOLLOWING PAGES)

IC 2163 DOES NOT HAVE ENOUGH ENERGY TO ESCAPE FROM THE GRAVITATIONAL GRASP OF NGC 2207

VISIBLE-LIGHT IMAGE

HUBBLE SPACE TELESCOPE (EARTH ORBITING)

25 MAY 1996
11 NOVEMBER 1998

114 MILLION LIGHT-YEARS FROM EARTH

GALAXY GROUP

GALAXIES ARE SCATTERED ACROSS the universe in a hierarchy of clusters. However, there are unusual collections of extremely tight-knit families of galaxies. Such a "compact group" is a small and relatively isolated system of typically four or five galaxies in close proximity.

Such groups do not form a distinct class, but may instead be extreme examples of tightly bound galactic systems. The first example was found over a century ago. Distinguishing such groups from the general galaxy background is so difficult that a second example wasn't found until some seventy years later. In 1982, astronomer Paul Hickson published a catalog of about a hundred such groups.

The galaxies in a suspected grouping must first be measured to see if they are at about the same distance from Earth. This is done by cosmological redshift. If they are at similar distances, they are likely close enough to gravitationally interact with one another.

Studying the star clusters and smaller galaxies inside compact groups provides insights into how galactic encounters may have driven galaxy evolution in the early universe. Galaxies interacted more often then because they were closer together.

THE GALAXIES IN THE HICKSON COMPACT GROUP (HCG 87) MOVE THROUGH SPACE TOGETHER DUE TO THEIR GRAVITATIONAL RELATIONSHIP

THE LARGE EDGE-ON SPIRAL ACROSS THE BOTTOM, THE FUZZY ELLIPTICAL TO ITS RIGHT AND THE SPIRAL AT TOP ARE KNOWN MEMBERS OF THE GROUP. THE SMALL SPIRAL IN THE MIDDLE IS PROBABLY A DISTANT OBJECT AND NOT PART OF THE GROUP.

VISIBLE-LIGHT IMAGE

GEMINI OBSERVATORY SOUTH 8M MIRROR TELESCOPE WITH GMOS

25 MAY 2003

400 MILLION LIGHT-YEARS FROM EARTH

LOCAL GROUP

TRIANGULUM GALAXY (M33) [RIGHT]

THE SMALLEST OF THE THREE LARGEST GALAXIES IN THE LOCAL GROUP

VISIBLE-LIGHT AND RADIO COMPOSITE

NSF 0.9M TELESCOPE AT KITT PEAK NATIONAL

OBSERVATORY, NOAO, WITH RADIO DATA FROM NRAO'S VERY LARGE ARRAY AND THE WESTERBORK SYNTHESIS RADIO TELESCOPE

12 JANUARY 2001

30,000 LIGHT-YEARS ACROSS

2 MILLION LIGHT-YEARS FROM EARTH

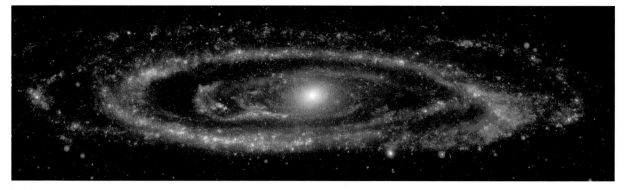

THE LOCAL GROUP IS THE NAME for our immediate neighborhood of approximately 36 galaxies. It is defined by a volume of space six million light-years across. Our group is a microcosm of the universe at large, having an estimated total mass equal to one trillion Suns. We are on the edge of the Local Supercluster of thousands of galaxies in the direction of the constellation Virgo.

The Local Group offers a sampler of the types of galaxies that populated the far more distant universe. Some of the smaller galaxies provide fossil evidence of how the universe evolved over the past 13 billion years. This is harbored in dwarf irregular galaxies, dwarf galaxies, globular clusters, and the complex architecture of the twin spiral giants The

Milky Way and Andromeda. There is even tentative but intriguing evidence that there might be a "dark galaxy," a cold clump of hydrogen and dark matter that has yet to form stars.

Over billions of years the Local Group has evolved from chaos to order through many collisions and mergers of small galaxies and star clusters. Computer simulations show what can only be described as a Cosmic Cuisinart. Smaller galaxies whip crazily around under gravity and merge to build up the halo, bulge and disk of the larger spiral galaxies. Most of the dwarfs are stretched and ripped apart by the gravitational tugs of their bigger neighbors.

The only forensic evidence of this violent cannibalistic past

lies in the halo of our galaxy. The assimilated remains from ripped-apart clusters shine there as wispy streams of stars that form contrails a hundred million light-years long. These visual clues suggest that the galaxy's halo is populated with older stars that formed in the Local Group billions of years ago.

The stars from one encounter are literally raining down onto our galactic neighborhood now. Other fragile dwarf galaxies show disruption as they venture close to the gravitational center of the vast Milky Way.

Embedded in the expanding and accelerating universe, the Local Group is expected to remain intact for trillions of years to come, though its galaxies will continue to evolve.

ANDROMEDA GALAXY (M 31) [ABOVE]

BLUE INDICATES HOT, HIGH-MASS STARS. GREEN DOTS ARE OLDER STARS. THE BRIGHT SPOT AT CENTER IS A DENSE POPULATION OF OLD STARS. RED MARKS AREAS OF STAR BIRTH.

ULTRAVIOLET AND INFRARED COMPOSITE

GALEX TELESCOPE (EARTH-ORBITING) SEPTEMBER, OCTOBER 2003

SPITZER SPACE TELESCOPE (EARTH-TRAILING SOLAR ORBIT) 25 AUGUST 2004

260,000 LIGHT-YEARS ACROSS

2.5 MILLION LIGHT-YEARS FROM EARTH

SATELLITE GALAXY

A SATELLITE GALAXY IS A SMALL galaxy that orbits a much larger galaxy like our Milky Way. Because these small galaxies are caught up in the gravitational web of the larger dominant galaxy, they may be assimilated by the larger galaxy or ripped apart by its tidal pull. Simulations show that the Milky Way probably grew out of collisions and mergers of smaller galaxies, which were more abundant in the early universe.

The Large Magellanic Cloud (LMC) is the nearest example of a satellite galaxy. It is the larger of a pair of fuzzy cloudlike objects easily visible in the Southern Hemisphere. The smaller one is the neighboring satellite galaxy called the Small Magellanic Cloud (SMC). The Portuguese navigator Ferdinand Magellan noted the "clouds" on his voyage around the world in the early 1500s. A recent theory suggests that the pair of Magellanic Clouds are interacting with our Milky Way's invisible dark matter to create a puzzling warp in our galaxy's disk.

The LMC is 160,000 light-years away. It is roughly 10,000 light-years across, or one-tenth the Milky Way's diameter. The LMC is irregular in shape except for a central bar of older stars. It is a firestorm of star birth, and therefore the nearest laboratory for studying how stars are born in clusters. The most massive of the Milky Way's satellite galaxies, the LMC is the site of the closest supernova in modern times, SN 1987A, which exploded on 23 February 1987.

A detailed look at the dust and gas clouds in the LMC is revealed in the infrared picture at right. Vast clouds of gas and dust can be found near young stars. They appear reddish in infrared false-color views. Dust is scattered unevenly between the stars and in shells around the old stars. Also discernible in the infrared are huge spacious caverns carved by gas outflows, energetic and blistering, from massive stars.

THE LARGE MAGELLANIC CLOUD, AN IRREGULAR SATELLITE GALAXY

BLUE: STARLIGHT FROM OLD STARS IN THE CENTRAL BAR
WHITE: HOT MASSIVE STARS BURIED IN DUST
RED: COOLER GAS AND DUST LIT BY AMBIENT STARLIGHT

INFRARED MOSAIC OF MORE THAN 100 TILES

SPITZER SPACE TELESCOPE (EARTH-TRAILING SOLAR ORBIT)

15–26 JULY, 26 OCTOBER–2 NOVEMBER 2005

163,000 LIGHT-YEARS FROM EARTH

OUT

THERE

SEEING THE WAY THINGS WERE

GRAVITATIONAL LENS

IMAGINE BEING SUSPENDED IN Earth's atmosphere and looking through a giant magnifying glass at the surface below. In space, there are natural occurrences that act as a magnifier or zoom lens. This phenomenon, called a gravitational lens, is a massive object, such as a large galaxy or galaxy cluster, that bends and magnifies the light of galaxies located far behind it.

But how does a gravitational lens work? How does it actually bend the light? Although light travels in a straight line, the direction is influenced by space. Most of the matter in space is dark matter, an invisible form that is the source of most gravity in the universe. The gravity of dark matter holds galaxy clusters together. According to Einstein's theory of general relativity, gravity warps and bends space, distorting a beam of light. So when light passes through the gravitational lens formed by a galaxy cluster, the light is distorted and bent. Although Einstein predicted the effects of gravity on light in space, he thought it would be difficult to observe them from Earth.

Science has known about gravitational lenses since the 1970s, but the Hubble Space Telescope has brought them into fine detail. The Hubble has used a gravitational lens to get a view of the distant universe by looking through the galaxy cluster known as Abell 1689, located 2.2 billion light-years away. Hubble astronomers have speculated that some of the objects in view are more than 13 billion light-years away.

The use of gravitational zoom lenses, like other cutting-edge explorations into what's out there, lets us see farther into the universe. And in a wonderful cosmic twist, the farther we see into space, the farther back in time we go.

THE CENTER OF GALAXY CLUSTER ABELL 1689 IS A GIANT MAGNIFYING GLASS IN SPACE

THIS GRAVITATIONAL LENS ENLARGES GALAXIES BILLIONS OF LIGHT-YEARS AWAY

VISIBLE-LIGHT IMAGE

HUBBLE SPACE TELESCOPE (EARTH-ORBITING)

JUNE 2002

2.2 BILLION LIGHT-YEARS FROM EARTH

DARK MATTER

WATER COVERS THREE-QUARTERS of Earth's surface. Just imagine how perplexed we would be if we didn't know what water was.

Scientists face a similar conundrum because four-fifths of the matter in the universe is of an unknown form. We can't even see it because it doesn't emit or reflect light. Whatever it is, it's not made out of the same stuff that stars, planets and even humans are made of: protons, electrons and neutrons. For want of a better description, it's simply called "dark matter."

How do astronomers know that dark matter exists at all? Its presence can be inferred from its gravitational tug on visible matter. The ghostly pull of dark matter controls the rotational speeds of galaxies, as well as the orbital motion of galaxies in clusters. It even traps hot gas inside such clusters, like a lid on a steaming kettle.

The gravity from dark matter also warps space like a funhouse mirror — it bends and amplifies the light of far more distant galaxies, just as a magnifying lens distorts your view. This phenomenon in space is called gravitational lensing.

The idea that some mass in the universe is "missing" was first proposed in 1933 by Swiss astrophysicist Fritz Zwicky.

While studying the Coma Cluster of galaxies, Zwicky estimated the cluster's total mass in stars. But the mass was not sufficient to hold the cluster together. The cluster would have so little "gravitational glue" from stars alone, that it would fly apart. Zwicky realized that there must be 400 times more mass present than could be accounted for by stars.

Critical new evidence for the reality of dark matter came from recent observations by NASA's Chandra X-ray Observatory, the Hubble Space Telescope and several ground-based observatories. They all examined the Bullet Cluster, the result of a violent collision of two smaller galactic clusters that happened 100 million years ago. The object gets its name from a pair of bullet-shaped clouds of superhot gas embedded inside the cluster.

Scientists were able to map the distribution of normal and dark matter in the Bullet Cluster's collision. Normal matter in the form of superheated gas (pink) was traced by X-rays. Dark matter (blue) was traced in visible light through gravitational lensing. Astronomers discovered that normal matter and dark matter had been pulled apart in the collision.

It would be like slamming two cars into a brick wall, one made of matter and the other of dark matter. The normal matter car would crash and deform as it hit the wall, while the dark matter car would sail on through as if the wall weren't there. This is exactly what astronomers found in the Bullet Cluster collision. The normal gas matter collided, was compressed and heated, while the dark matter kept on sailing through the collision.

In 2007 astronomers released the first large-scale three-dimensional map of dark matter in the universe. The map provides the best evidence yet that normal matter — stars and galaxies — collects within the densest concentrations of dark matter.

It was like seeing the tree under its Christmas lights. Astronomers used the Hubble Space Telescope's images of gravitational lensing to map out the concentration of dark matter in space. When the map of dark matter was compared with other astronomical observations, it became clear that stars are positioned where dark matter congregates. In essence, dark matter is the scaffolding inside of which stars and galaxies have been assembled over billions of years.

DIRECT PROOF OF DARK MATTER IN THE BULLET GALAXY CLUSTER (1E 0657-556)

GRAVITATIONAL LENSING TRACES DARK MATTER IN THE CLUMPS OF BLUE. X-RAYS TRACE NORMAL MATTER IN CLUMPS OF PINK.

X-RAY AND VISIBLE-LIGHT COMPOSITE

X-RAY: CHANDRA X-RAY OBSERVATORY

VISIBLE LIGHT: HUBBLE SPACE TELESCOPE, ESO 2M WIDE-FIELD IMAGER, 6.5M MAGELLAN TELESCOPE

OCTOBER 2003– OCTOBER 2004

3.4 BILLION LIGHT-YEARS FROM EARTH

GEMS SURVEY

THIS COLLECTION OF GALACTIC jewels, a mosaic of 70 images, is a tool for studying the formation of the universe. The images were taken from a much larger photograph, the GEMS Survey. That remarkable composite image of 40,000 galaxies in the constellation Fornax was pieced together from 78 separate exposures taken by the Hubble Space Telescope's Advanced Camera for Surveys. Even though the GEMS photograph is the largest color image Hubble has ever produced, it covers only a small piece of the sky — about the size of an aspirin tablet held at arm's length.

The survey (GEMS is an acronym for Galaxy Evolution from Morphology and SEDs, or Spectral Energy Distributions) seeks to determine the relative age, evolution and relationships of the galaxies that make up the universe. Images of the most distant galaxies allow scientists to see back in time some nine billion years. Among the questions they hope to answer is how gravitational forces affect the formation, merger and evolution of galaxies. They are also studying the role of stellar bars, concentrations of stars that affect the course of galaxy formation by pushing gas toward the galactic center, which can result in the birth of new stars.

GEMS SURVEY
GALAXY EVOLUTION
FROM MORPHOLOGY AND
SPECTRAL ENERGY
DISTRIBUTIONS

VISIBLE-LIGHT MOSAIC
OF SELECT GALAXIES FROM
THE SURVEY

HUBBLE SPACE TELESCOPE
OPERATED BY THE SPACE
TELESCOPE SCIENCE
INSTITUTE; OBSERVING
PROGRAM: MAX-PLANCK-
INSTITUTE FOR ASTRONOMY

AUGUST 2002–
MARCH 2003

100 MILLION–10 BILLION
LIGHT-YEARS FROM EARTH

HYDROGEN SKY

HYDROGEN IS ALL AROUND US. The primordial element has been the main component of the universe since the Big Bang. This all-sky hydrogen survey maps the distribution of hydrogen atoms across the entire Milky Way Galaxy.

"Hydrogen makes up the atmosphere of galaxies," says Dr Jay Lockman of the National Radio Astronomy Observatory at Green Bank, West Virginia. This atmosphere, or interstellar medium, is both the source of clouds that create new stars and the repository of gas outflow from existing stars. The atmosphere is much more extensive than the visible Milky Way. It governs the future of our galaxy by determining where new stars will form and what their composition will be.

A neutral hydrogen atom is made up of a proton and an electron, each of which spins like a top on its axis. In its lowest energy state, the particles spin in opposite directions. But occasionally the atom will collide with another, flipping the electron's spin to a higher energy state. After a few million years, the electron will spontaneously flip back. When it does, it emits a radio

**ALL-SKY HYDROGEN MAP,
WITH THE PLANE OF THE
MILKY WAY GALAXY RUNNING
THROUGH THE CENTER**

RADIO IMAGE (COLOR ADDED)

NATIONAL RADIO ASTRONOMY
OBSERVATORY, GREEN BANK

PARKES RADIO OBSERVATORY

BELL LABORATORIES,
CRAWFORD HILL

UNIVERSITY OF CALIFORNIA
AT BERKELEY, HAT CREEK

1970S–1980S

A FEW LIGHT-YEARS TO 100,000
LIGHT-YEARS FROM EARTH

wave. Although this process is extremely slow, there are so many hydrogen atoms in the Milky Way that their collective radio signal is easily detected on modern radio telescopes.

The presence of hydrogen is most intense along the galactic plane (color coded in red). The high density of hydrogen can lead to the creation of new stars, for a star like our Sun is mostly hydrogen. It is estimated that one star a year is formed from the clouds of hydrogen in the Milky Way. At the other end of the star cycle, the wavelike cloud structures (above, left of center) show evidence of massive clusters of stars gone supernova.

The continuing study of neutral hydrogen could be important in locating dark matter. Scientists measuring the velocity of hydrogen far from the galactic plane found that it is gravitationally bound to a large amount of matter. This mysterious matter was originally called missing mass; but the mass was not missing, because the hydrogen reacted to its gravitational tug. What was missing was its light — hence the name dark matter.

INFRARED CIRRUS

TO THE NAKED EYE, VAST stretches of sky appear dark and empty – a velvet backdrop against which the movements of planets and stars can be read. But space is not empty. The infrared cirrus is found in nearly every direction. A surprise discovery in the late 20th century was that the "invisible void" is filled with wispy clouds of gas – mostly hydrogen and helium – and dust. The fine particulate dust is mainly made of carbon, silicon and oxygen.

The amorphous structures have been named infrared cirrus because they resemble the cirrus clouds in Earth's atmosphere and can be detected only through infrared light. A mixture of intense cold and slight heat is the reason infrared cirrus can be seen only in this wavelength. It is a cosmic deep freeze with temperatures as low as −400 °F (−240 °C). Only a little bit of warmth, provided by visible and ultraviolet light from nearby stars, is efficiently absorbed by the dust. The dust re-radiates the absorbed energy, which can be seen only in infrared.

The emissions of infrared cirrus help scientists understand the structure of our galaxy. The current consensus is that the Milky Way is a barred spiral galaxy. The bar has a strong concentration of gas and dust that provides most of the emission we see in the above image.

The density of this interstellar substance varies throughout space. It can be dispersed in a supernova blast. It can be blown about by interstellar winds. And it can gather together in more crowded areas called nebulas. Infrared cirrus is the recycling material of stars — both the residue of stellar explosions and the raw ingredients that form new stars.

INFRARED CIRRUS

THE "EMPTY AREAS" BETWEEN STARS ARE FILLED WITH DUST THAT CANNOT BE SEEN IN VISIBLE LIGHT

INFRARED IMAGE

MSX SATELLITE (NEAR SUN-SYNCHRONOUS ORBIT)

24 APRIL 1996–20 FEBRUARY 1997

15,000–18,000 LIGHT-YEARS FROM EARTH

WMAP

EVER SINCE THE BIG BANG THEORY of the universe came into wide-spread acceptance, scientists have been trying to understand how the universe evolved from a seething soup of particles into the sea of planets, stars and galaxies around us today. In 2003, in a highly sophisticated

variant on one of the basic rules of space observation — that the light we perceive in the sky is light traveling toward us out of the past — NASA's Wilkinson Microwave Anisotropy Probe (WMAP) succeeded in producing the first detailed full-sky map of the universe at the dawn of time.

A "baby picture" of the 13-billion-year-old universe at 379,000 years, it is both a powerful confirmation of the basic theory of Big Bang and the first record of light freely emerging from a dense fireball that expanded from the Big Bang.

Much as an infrared weather

map of Earth displays the distribution of heat and cold in a clear, discernible pattern, the WMAP image captures the distri-bution of light just a few hun-dred thousand years after the Big Bang. As the universe continued to cool, protons and electrons combined to form

WMAP LOOKS BACK IN TIME TO WHEN LIGHT FIRST APPEARED – 379,000 YEARS AFTER THE BIG BANG

MICROWAVE IMAGE

WILKINSON MICROWAVE ANISOTROPY PROBE (ORBIT 1 MILLION MILES/ 1.6 MILLION KM FROM EARTH OPPOSITE THE SUN)

MARCH 2006 (FOURTH FULL-SKY SCAN COMPLETE)

PROBE TO INFINITY

neutral hydrogen, whose inter-action with cosmic microwave background photons made the WMAP image possible across billions of light-years.

Working from WMAP's radia-tion "blueprint" of the universe, where red signifies "warmer" spots and blue "cooler" areas,

cosmologists have been able to identify the faint precursors of galaxies, as if reading an adult's ultimate physical dimensions and contours from the cells of a week-old fetus.

Data provided by WMAP have helped scientists confirm or refine many assumptions about

the universe, beginning with its composition, now determined to be 4 percent atoms, 22 percent cold dark matter and 74 percent dark energy.

The white lines in this updated 2006 image measure the polar-ization of light immediately after the Big Bang. By analyzing the

polarizaton, WMAP found evi-dence that inflation occurred in the early universe. The universe's rate of expansion has been nar-rowed to within a 5 percent mar-gin of error, a factor crucial to cal-culating its age, which has been newly fixed at 13.7 billion years, within a 1 percent margin of error.

THE LIVING COLOR UNIVERSE

The Science Behind the Images   by Ray Villard

MORE THAN ANY OTHER SCIENCE, astronomy relies on the art of seeing. The ephemeral photons of starlight are every bit as valuable to astronomers as fossils to paleontologists, or rock core samples to geologists. Because celestial objects beyond our solar system are physically unreachable, everything we know about them is encoded in starlight. Knowledge about any astronomical object is deduced from its brightness, shape, sky position and, most important of all, color.

On a clear night the stars simply look like pinpoints of white light, and the sky we see is largely devoid of color. However, a careful observer will notice that some stars have pastel shades of blue, yellow or orange. In fact, the name of the summer star Antares means "rival of Mars" because its orange hue mimics the ruddy glow of the red planet.

The universe is intrinsically much more vibrant with color than these muted shades. Our eyes simply cannot detect the rich colors spread across the canvas of the universe. There is too little energy in feeble starlight – which has traveled hundreds or thousands of light-years across space – to stimulate the red, green and blue receptors in our retina. These cone cells communicate color information to our brain's vision center, where information is combined into a color image. The more sensitive rod cells of the retina continue to faithfully capture photons to give us a black-and-white view on a dim night.

To capture these colors, we need telescopes that greatly amplify starlight. Much more than simply aesthetics, astronomical colors yield clues to a celestial object's chemical makeup, temperature, motion through space and even distance from Earth. Planet colors are the most natural and the easiest to interpret. Planets do not glow but simply reflect light from the Sun, just like any landscape on Earth. Planet colors are due to absorption of some wavelengths of light. The cyan hues of Neptune and Uranus are due to methane in their atmospheres, which absorbs red light. Mars's ruddy hue is due to a rusty iron-oxide soil that absorbs green wavelengths. Jupiter's Easter-egg look may come from sulfur compounds in the turbulent atmosphere. This process is no different from when we look at a green leaf. The chlorophyll absorbs red light. Hence the leaf looks green.

Anyone who has ever watched a fireworks display knows that extremely hot objects make light

THE ELECTROMAGNETIC SPECTRUM
Photographing the cosmos in different wavelengths of light allows us to explore otherwise "invisible" objects.

Milky Way in Gamma Rays

and color. Color, in fact, can be used to infer a star's temperature. Just watch as the coil in a toaster oven heats from dull cherry red to yellow-orange. Or imagine a dying ember fading from orange down to dull red. The cooler the star, the redder it is. Conversely, the hotter the star, the bluer it is. Color pictures of galaxies faithfully reveal the temperatures of these different stellar populations. The outer disk is rich in young hot blue stars. The older surviving stars in a galaxy's central bulge are more yellowish.

Interstellar clouds of glowing gas look like the neon lights on a honky-tonk strip of nightclubs.

When electrified, the gas neon glows a vibrant yellow; other gases also glow at specific colors. The colors are very saturated and pure. Likewise, gases in space are excited into glowing by being trapped and heated in magnetic fields, blasted by ultraviolet radiation and shocked by collisions with blast waves from exploding stars. Some of the rich colors are from elements that are fundamental to life on Earth. Oxygen glows deep blue, nitrogen is forest green, various energized states of hydrogen can cause it to glow magenta or green, sulfur glows yellow.

The process of producing color

images involves collecting energy from across the visible portion of the electromagnetic spectrum. Photographic film, video cameras and even the offset printing process all make color pictures by combining separate channels of color information. For example, film has three layers of photosensitive emulsion: red, green and blue. The balances between these primary colors can yield literally millions of hues. For purity and control of color, the motion picture industry developed the Technicolor process in the 1930s. Three separate rolls of black-and-white film were exposed simultaneously through red, blue and

green filters. The black-and-white strips were then projected through the same color filters and printed simultaneously onto a single piece of color film.

Likewise, spacecraft cameras take images through different colored filters. The overlap between some of these filters allows for a truly full-color spectrum image to be assembled. But scientists also need a wide assortment of narrow-band filters that are precisely tuned to certain frequencies of light. For example, the rarefied hot hydrogen in active regions on the Sun glows at a wavelength of 6562 angstroms (an angstrom is one 10-billionth of a meter). Like

Milky Way in X-Rays

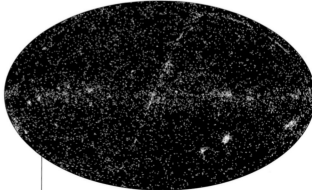

Milky Way in Ultraviolet

a radio station channel, a filter can be "fine-tuned" to block out extraneous color wavelengths and show detailed structure.

Some of the cameras that have returned the most spectacular pictures – Hubble's Advanced Camera for Surveys, the Mars rover cameras, the Cassini orbiter camera at Saturn – all have literally dozens of color filters for scientific analysis. These filters are used for precisely dissecting the colors of the universe from either glowing gases or reflected light.

The challenge for the science image processor is to combine all this information into an image that is a reasonable representation of reality. The rules for making an effective scientific picture are no different from the rules for an aesthetic photographic image. The image requires proper tonal range, from coal black to snow white. The full range of colors along the visible spectrum should be represented. Color, even artificially added to a monochrome image, provides an extra dimension for analyzing scientific details.

When digital imaging processing began to be used by astronomers in the 1970s, they applied artificial colors to the images. Gray tones could be assigned various hues. This made for some garish but scientifically meaningful space pictures through the 1980s. Now cameras have become more sophisticated, and microcomputers have allowed for more complex digital image processing, where color can be controlled even more precisely.

Still, the act of assembling an image sent back to Earth from a spacecraft or gleaned from a telescope will always require an element of subjectivity and interpretation by the science image processor. The first close-up images sent back to Earth by the Pioneer 10 spacecraft in the early 1970s were tweaked in a seat-of-the-pants style by a specialist who reasoned that Jupiter's ammonia ice crystal clouds should look white, just as they do in ground-based telescopes. When the first Viking lander touched down on Mars in 1976, imaging specialists adjusted the sky to be blue because they expected the sky to be deep blue, like our thin atmosphere as seen from an airplane at 20,000 feet (6,000m). Further calibration revealed, embarrassingly, that the Martian sky was a pinkish salmon color!

Another daunting challenge is that the universe is also vibrant in what can only be called "invisible colors," those energies along the

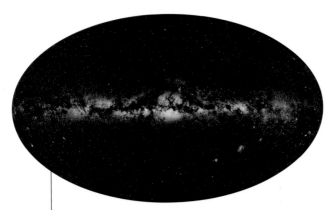

Milky Way in Visible Light

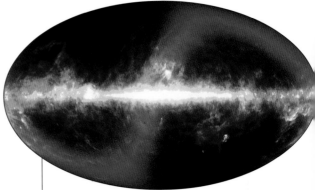

Milky Way in Infrared

electromagnetic spectrum that are beyond the visible wavelengths we call light. Infrared light comes from warm dust, radio waves come from interstellar gases, X-ray energies come from seething plasma heated to millions of degrees as it spirals into a black hole or gets sizzled by other violent phenomena. The only difference among these energies is the wavelengths of the radiation, just as the range of octaves on a piano all come from the same physical instrument.

Light is analogous to sound, which is also transmitted by waves. Our ears can hear from long-wavelength bass tones all the way up to ear-piecing short frequencies. However, our eyes see just a small midrange of electromagnetic wavelengths, which we call visible light. Without the power of telescopes, trying to comprehend the vibrancy of the electromagnetic universe is as impossible as trying to appreciate the richness of an orchestra through a small pocket radio speaker that can't reproduce bass or treble.

Obviously, wavelengths such as X-ray, radio and infrared do not have any colors detectable by the human eye. The image processor must pull these data into the world of visual perception by arbitrarily assigning colors to "invisible" light. For example, if pictures are taken at different infrared wavelengths, red, green and blue can be assigned to relatively long, medium and short wavelengths of light. This can produce gorgeous pictures that attempt to map color values onto invisible radiation. The artificial color can be obvious when all the stars look pink or blue. Likewise, X-ray intensities can be mapped onto colors to produce even more garish but scientifically meaningful images.

As remarkable as the human brain is, and as perfectly as the eye performs, our vision of the infinitely vast universe is greatly restricted. Telescopes, combined with computers and the talents of image-processing specialists, vastly expand our perception of the richness of the universe. Today's astronomical images are the most exquisite views of the universe humans have ever assembled. These images not only talk to us on a scientific, intellectual level, but also evoke emotions about the vibrancy and evocative beauty of deep space. Many of the celestial objects in this book appear as they did long ago and far away, so our only intimacy with them will always come exclusively through the sheer power of the color image.

Milky Way in Microwaves

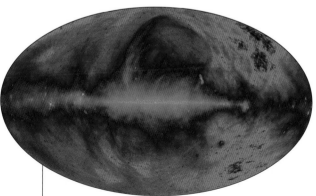

Milky Way in Radio Waves

THE IMAGE MAKERS
The Mechanical and Human Heroes of Space Exploration

EARTH-BASED

ANGLO-AUSTRALIAN OBSERVATORY

The 3.9m Anglo-Australian Telescope (AAT), located in New South Wales, Australia, went into operation in 1974. Until then, most of the world's largest telescopes were built in the Northern Hemisphere. The AAT was designed to explore some of the most exciting regions of the southern sky. The telescope's imaging camera once used special black-and-white photographic plates, now replaced by electronic detectors. Color images are created by combining three separate black-and-white exposures that record images in blue, green and red light.

CANADA-FRANCE-HAWAII TELESCOPE

Operational in 1979, the Canada-France-Hawaii Telescope (CFHT) is a 3.6m mirror optical/infrared telescope. The observatory is on the summit of Mauna Kea on the island of Hawaii. CFHT was originally designed for use with large photographic plates, but today employs a state-of-the-art MegaPrime optical 340-megapixel MegaCam digital camera system with a field of view (one degree by one degree) equal to the size of four full Moons.

EUROPEAN SOUTHERN OBSERVATORY

The flagship of the European Southern Observatory (ESO) is the Very Large Telescope (VLT), a series of four interconnected 8.2m reflecting telescopes. Placed in a trapezoidal configuration, the VLT is located on the summit of Cerro Paranal in Chile's Atacama desert. Each unit is housed in a thermally controlled building with a dome that can rotate independently or synchronously with the other

Canada-France-Hawaii Telescope

three telescopes. The first ESO facility, on top of Chile's La Silla mountain, is one of the world's most productive observing sites.

GEMINI OBSERVATORY

The multinational Gemini Observatory consists of twin 8m telescopes that are among the largest on Earth. They are located in each hemisphere in order to provide complete sky coverage. The Gemini North Telescope is on Hawaii's Mauna Kea. The Gemini South Telescope is on Cerro Pachón in the Chilean Andes. The Gemini telescopes excel in a variety of optical and infrared capabilities and incorporate adaptive optics to take the "twinkle" out of starlight.

MAGELLAN TELESCOPES

The twin Walter Baade and Landon Clay are 6.5m Magellan telescopes located at Las Campanas Observatory high in Chile's Atacama Desert. The

main mirrors are f/1.25 paraboloids, a radical change from traditional single-mirror designs. The twins are operated collaboratively by the Carnegie Institution, the University of Arizona, Harvard University, the University of Michigan and the Massachusetts Institute of Technology. The Giant Magellan Telescope, to be completed in 2016, will have a primary mirror with ten times the resolution of the Hubble Space Telescope.

NOAO

Kitt Peak National Observatory (KPNO), part of the National Optical Astronomy Observatory (NOAO), supports the most diverse collection of astronomical observatories on Earth for nighttime optical and infrared astronomy and daytime study of the Sun. The WIYN Observatory (a consortium which consists of the University of Wisconsin, Indiana University, Yale University and the NOAO) now operates the 0.9m and 3.5m telescopes. The Cerro Tololo Inter-American Observatory in Chile is also part of NOAO.

Chandra

NRAO

The U.S. National Radio Astronomy Observatory (NRAO) of the U.S. National Science Foundation designs, builds and operates several state-of-the-art radio telescopes. NRAO's Green Bank Telescope (GBT), a 100m radio telescope in West Virginia, is the largest movable man-made structure on Earth. The GBT is extremely sensitive to radio waves due to its huge parabolic dish, a mosaic of 2,004 movable aluminum panels.

NRAO's Very Large Array (VLA) is one of the world's premier radio observatories. It consists of 27 movable radio antennas in a Y-shaped configuration on the plains of New Mexico in the U.S.

NRAO also works on cooperative experiments with other observatories around the world.

Australia's 64m Parkes Radio Observatory is the first big-dish antenna telescope in the Southern Hemisphere. It has played a vital role in studying quasars and discovered the first pulsars outside the Milky Way. During the APOLLO 11 mission in 1969, Parkes received the first TV signals from the Moon's surface and is still active in receiving radio signals for human and robotic missions of NASA (National Aeronautics and Space Administration) of the U.S.

The Westerbork Synthesis Radio Telescope in the Netherlands consists of 14 dish-shaped antennas, enabling the study of phenomena such as pulsars, the motions of galaxies and black holes.

The 20-foot microwave satellite "horn antenna" on New Jersey's Crawford Hill in the U.S. was used by Bell Laboratories in 1965 to detect the first evidence of cosmic background radiation, the afterglow of the Big Bang.

PALOMAR OBSERVATORY

Completed in 1948, the Samuel Oschin 48-inch Schmidt telescope at the Palomar Observatory in California surveys large areas of the northern sky. One of its first projects (in 1950) was to photograph the whole visible sky in both blue and red light. A companion survey was completed in the Southern Hemisphere with a companion Schmidt telescope operated by the United Kingdom. In the 1980s, thousands of 14-inch-square (36cm) glass plates were digitized to make a catalog of stars for the Hubble Space Telescope.

SWEDISH 1M SOLAR TELESCOPE

The Swedish 1m Solar Telescope (SST) is operated by the Royal Swedish Academy of Sciences' Institute for Solar Physics. The optical telescope is the largest of its kind in Europe. Located atop an extinct volcano on the Canary Islands, the SST boasts an adaptive mirror that shifts its shape 1,000 times a second to adjust to the rapidly changing distortions in the Sun's image. As a result, it can see features as small as 43 miles (70km) on the Sun's surface.

2MASS

The Two Micron All Sky Survey (2MASS), a 10-year collaboration between the University of Massachusetts, NASA and the U.S. National Science Foundation, produced an atlas of the entire sky in infrared light. Because infrared radiation streams through interstellar clouds, the 2MASS survey has revealed stars in the farthest reaches of our galaxy and in parts of the universe that were previously obscured. The survey has catalogued half a billion celestial objects. The Northern Hemisphere telescope is in Arizona, the southern one at Chile's Cerro Tololo Inter-American Observatory.

NEAR-EARTH

CHANDRA X-RAY OBSERVATORY

The Chandra X-Ray Observatory is named after the late Indian-American Nobel laureate, Subrahmanyan Chandrasekhar, who was known as Chandra ("moon" or "luminous" in Sanskrit). Launched by NASA in 1999, Chandra is an advanced X-ray observatory, resulting in images 25 times sharper than the best previous X-ray telescope. It provides images of the high-energy universe of black holes, neutron stars and hot gases.

SOHO

GALEX

NASA's Galaxy Evolution Explorer (GALEX) is an orbiting telescope that surveys galaxies and stars in ultraviolet light across 10 billion years of cosmic history. Such observations tell scientists how galaxies evolve and change. GALEX probes the causes of star formation during a period when most of the stars and the elements had their origins. Launched in April 2003, the large, circular field of view of the GALEX telescope allows astronomers to observe the whole sky and to study hundreds of thousands of galaxies.

HUBBLE SPACE TELESCOPE

Designed in the 1970s and launched in 1990, the NASA/ESA (European Space Agency) Hubble Space Telescope (HST) is currently the largest optical-UV observatory in space. At 360 miles (580km) above Earth's blurry atmosphere, Hubble sees the universe ten times sharper than most larger ground-based telescopes. Named for American astronomer Edwin Hubble, who confirmed the expanding universe, the telescope can detect objects down to one 10-billionth the sensitivity of the human eye. HST has four onboard cameras that view the universe from ultraviolet to near-infrared wavelengths. Three use CCD (charge-coupled device) arrays: the Space Telescope Imaging Spectrograph (STIS), the Wide Field and Planetary Camera 2 (WFPC2) and the Advanced Camera for Surveys (ACS).

LANDSAT SATELLITES

In order to study Earth's evolving landscape, NASA launched a series of six Landsat satellites beginning in 1972. Landsat 5 and Landsat 7 are still gathering remotely sensed images of the continents and coastal regions under the management of the United States Geological Survey (USGS). Both satellites operate in a polar orbit at an altitude of about 44 miles (705km). The Landsat thematic mapper sensors measure reflected sunlight in visible and infrared light. The various wavelengths allow for the characterization of land cover, and the USGS historical archive provides the ability to track changes in land cover and land use over time.

MSX SATELLITE

Launched in 1996, the U.S. Ballistic Missile Defense Organization's Midcourse Space Experiment (MSX) was a 5,950-pound (2,700-k) satellite in a 560-mile (900-km) near-Sun synchronous orbit. MSX was equipped with a cooled infrared sensor to detect and track missile test warheads. The sensor was also used to collect more than 200 gigabytes of data on celestial backgrounds during the 10 months that cryogen was able to keep the sensor cold. Another objective was to map the entire galactic plane in the mid-infrared. Since the coolant evaporated, sensors on board have been used to locate space debris that has been lost by ground-based radar.

POLAR SPACECRAFT

NASA's Polar spacecraft was launched in 1996 to obtain space environment data from high above Earth's poles. The satellite is in an elliptical orbit, where it swings down to the altitude at which auroras occur and then out to the Van Allen radiation belts that encircle Earth. Polar's instruments observe space particles as they follow Earth's magnetic field and subsequently fluoresce oxygen and nitrogen to create the auroras.

SHUTTLE RADAR TOPOGRAPHY MISSION

During an 11-day Space Shuttle mission in February 2000, radar measurements were collected from over 80 percent of Earth's land mass – home to 95 percent of the world's population. A cooperative project between the U.S., Germany and Italy, the Shuttle Radar Topography Mission (SRTM) produced the first detailed, near-global model of Earth's landforms. Radar can

WMAP

"see" through clouds, so SRTM was equipped for mapping areas often obscured, such as the tropics. By measuring depth or surface height, SRTM captured the dimension that is missing in most flat satellite images. When satellite images are now merged with SRTM elevation data, Earth's three-dimensional surface can be mapped by computer in stereoscopic and perspective views.

SOHO SPACECRAFT
The NASA/ESA Solar and Heliospheric Observatory (SOHO) is the most complex observatory ever built to study the Sun. Launched in 1995, it is located at a gravitational balancing position, called a Lagrangian point, nearly one million miles (1.6 million km) from Earth and 92 million miles (148 million km) from the Sun. Among its 12 instruments are: the Extreme Ultraviolet Imaging Telescope (EIT); the Large Angle and Spectrometric Coronagraph (LASCO), a set of three telescopes designed to block light coming from the solar disk in

order to see the fainter emissions from the corona; the Michelson Doppler Imager (MDI) that studies the interior of the Sun; and the Solar Ultraviolet Measurements of Emitted Radiation (SUMER) telescope and spectrometer that observe the Sun's spectra, coronal holes and active regions.

SPITZER SPACE TELESCOPE
NASA's Spitzer Space Telescope (SST), named after American astronomer Lyman Spitzer, Jr., was launched in 2003. SST explores the skeletal universe by seeing objects of infrared energy that radiate through dusty space. By penetrating vast, dense clouds of gas and dust, Spitzer can examine star-forming regions, the centers of galaxies, and newly forming planetary systems that are hidden from optical telescopes. The SST has an 0.85m mirror that beams light to three instruments cryogenically cooled to near absolute zero so the telescope can observe infrared signals from space without interference from its own heat.

TERRA SATELLITE
Terra, Latin for land, is the flagship satellite in NASA's Earth-observing system. Launched in 1999, Terra's goal is to assess the health of the planet by providing data about land, oceans, ice, atmosphere and life. From its orbital vantage point of 440 miles (710km), Terra observes the entire planet every one to two days and flies in near formation with Landsat 7 to provide cross-comparative data.

TRACE SATELLITE
The Transition Region and Coronal Explorer (TRACE) satellite explores the three-dimensional magnetic structures that rise above the surface of the Sun and into its upper atmosphere. The 30cm telescope aperture collects sunlight, and the primary and secondary mirrors select ultraviolet, extreme-ultraviolet and visible light for imaging. A CCD detector captures a view of about one-twentieth of the solar disk with each observation.

WMAP
NASA's Wilkinson Microwave Anisotropy Probe (WMAP) has made the sharpest image to date of the entire universe as it appeared shortly after the Big Bang. Named in honor of David Wilkinson of Princeton University, WMAP was launched in 2001 and maintains an orbit about a million miles (1.6 million km) from Earth. The spacecraft has a pair of back-to-back telescopes that focus the microwave radiation from two spots on nearly opposite parts of the sky. As the spacecraft spins, the telescopes sweep out a Spirograph pattern of the sky. Over the course of a year, this pattern fills in to make a complete map of the universe.

YOHKOH
The Yohkoh satellite, an observatory launched in 1991, was a mission of Japan's Institute of Space and Astronomical Science (ISAS), with support from U.S. and U.K. scientists. Through its

Mars Express

two imagers and two spectro-meters, Yohkoh ("sunbeam") observed solar flares in X-rays and gamma rays. Information about the temperature and densi-ty of the plasma emitting the X-rays was obtained by compar-ing images through filters of dif-ferent wavelengths.

SPACECRAFT, PROBES AND CAMERAS

APOLLO 12 / APOLLO 17 HANDHELD 70MM HASSELBLADS

Between 1968 and 1972, Apollo astronauts made more than 18,000 color and black-and-white still images with the Swedish-made Hasselblad EL (electric) camera, each with a Zeiss Planar 60mm or 500mm lens. Adapted for use in both the vacuum of space and Apollo's pressurized cabins, the cameras were battery-powered, semi-automatic and, for most lunar surface exploration, attached to the astronauts' pressure suits at chest height. The cameras used detachable 70mm maga-zines and Kodak SO368

Ektachrome MS (ASA 64) and 3401 PlusXX (ASA 80-125) black-and-white film. To save weight on the return voyage, most of the cameras and lenses were left at the landing site.

CASSINI-HUYGENS

Cassini-Huygens is a joint NASA/ESA/ASI (Italian Space Agency) mission that will study Saturn, its many rings and its moons. After a seven-year, two-billion-mile (3.2-billion-km) journey, Cassini- Huygens entered the ringed planet's orbit in 2004. The tour is programmed to last at least four years and will involve about 75 orbits, with flybys of many of Saturn's moons, especially the haze-engulfed moon Titan. The space-craft consisted of the Cassini orbiter and the Huygens probe. The probe descended via para-chute onto Titan, Saturn's biggest moon, in January 2005, sending data to Cassini, which beamed them to Earth. Cassini has two cameras, a wide-angle and a narrow-angle, both fitted with nearly two dozen filters from ultraviolet to infrared.

CLEMENTINE

The Clementine mission, launched in 1994, was a joint project of the U.S. Strategic Defense Initiative Organization (SDIO) and NASA. Lunar map-ping took place over approxi-mately two months. The obser-vations included imaging at var-ious wavelengths to assess the surface mineralogy of the Moon. The High-Resolution Camera consisted of a telescope with an image intensifier and a CCD imager. Clementine also had two star tracker cameras that imaged background stars to help navigate the spacecraft. Its broadband capabilities were limited to imaging dim targets such as the lunar surface illumi-nated by earthshine.

DEEP IMPACT

The Deep Impact space probe performed the first mission to explore the interior of a comet by releasing a speeding im-pactor into the side of comet Tempel 1. On July Fourth 2005,

Deep Impact's battery-powered projectile and the comet drove into each other at 20,000 miles (32,000km) an hour, colliding in a fireworks spectacular. The strike into Tempel 1's nucleus was captured in pictures by the impactor, the probe and tele-scopes in space and on Earth to study the icy debris blasted off the comet, as well as the pris-tine interior material exposed by the impact.

GALILEO

NASA's Galileo, the first space-craft to orbit one of the outer planets, was launched in 1989. The spacecraft made 34 orbits of Jupiter during its 14-year mission, making numerous fly-bys of the four largest moons – Europa, Ganymede, Callisto and Io. The camera optics were built around a 1,500mm focal length narrow-angle telescope that was originally built for Voyager. The wavelength range extended from the visible to the near-infrared. At the heart of the imaging system was a CCD detector with a filter wheel for taking color pictures. Galileo

Lunar Orbiter 4

was intentionally destroyed in Jupiter's atmosphere in 2003 to prevent contamination of its moon Europa.

LUNAR ORBITER 4

NASA conducted five Lunar Orbiter missions in 1966–1967. Their purpose was to map the lunar surface in preparation for the manned APOLLO landings. The orbiters photographed 99 percent of the Moon and could see objects as small as a card table. The first three missions imaged 20 potential landing sites. Lunar Orbiter 4 photographed the entire near side and 95 percent of the farside. The orbiter's dual-lens camera system recorded about 550 high- and medium-resolution frames on 70mm black-and-white film. The film was chemically processed in an onboard mini-photo lab. An optical scanner read areas of light and dark on the film emulsion and radioed the data to Earth as a continuous analog video signal, where it was exposed onto strips of photographic paper and assembled into a lunar portrait.

MAGELLAN

NASA's Magellan, named after the 16th-century Portuguese explorer who first circumnavigated the Earth, was launched in 1989. It was the first spacecraft to do detailed imaging of the surface of Venus from orbit. During the first eight months, Magellan collected radar images of 98 percent of the planet's surface. Because of the dense, opaque atmosphere, Magellan's Synthetic Aperture Radar (SAR) system used bursts of microwave energy, somewhat like a camera flash, to illuminate the planet's surface. The SAR system was also used to collect altimetry data showing the elevations of various surface features and allowing for three-dimensional images.

MARINER 10

In 1973, NASA's Mariner 10 became the first spacecraft to visit the innermost planet Mercury. It was also the first probe to use gravity assist, a means of propulsion that uses the gravity of one planet to help propel the craft to another — in this case, Venus to Mercury. Mariner had a sunshade that was deployed after launch to protect it on the Sun side. Louvers on the electronics compartments also helped control interior temperatures. The camera system consisted of two Cassegrain telescopes with eight filters. The imaging was done with a pair of vidicon tube cameras that could take narrow- and wide-angle images.

MARS EXPRESS

The European Space Agency's Mars Express entered into orbit around Mars in 2003. Mars Express is designed to map the subsurface aquifers that may have carved the gully and channel features on Mars. The High Resolution Stereo Camera (HRSC) images the planet in full color. Separate exposures can be combined to make a 3-D image, revealing details as small as a golf cart. In 2004, Mars Express confirmed the existence of water ice in the south polar cap region.

MARS GLOBAL SURVEYOR

NASA's Mars Global Surveyor (MGS), which entered a low-altitude polar orbit in 1997, completed its primary mission in 2001. Extending its mission until 2006, MGS circled Mars longer than any other spacecraft. It studied the entire Martian surface and atmosphere, and returned more data about the red planet than all previous missions combined. The camera system collected images on a CCD array, stored them on board as digital files and then transmitted them to Earth. One camera had a wide-angle lens that produced a daily image of Mars. The other, a narrow-angle lens, captured images of objects as small as a car.

2001 MARS ODYSSEY

Since 2001, NASA's Mars Odyssey has mapped the chemical elements and minerals that make up the Martian surface. Its goals include looking for rocks altered by water and hot spots

Stardust

indicating underground hydro-thermal activity. The imaging system, THEMIS (Thermal Emission Imaging System), contains two independent multispectral systems. The optics focus light onto the infrared and visible detectors. A thermal infrared imager can resolve objects almost 1,000 feet (305m) long, and a visible imager can resolve objects the size of a house.

MARS RECONNAISSANCE ORBITER

This spacecraft launched in 2005 will study the history of water on Mars by inspecting the surface, monitoring the atmosphere and probing underground. Other missions have demonstrated that water once flowed on the planet, but it is unknown if the liquid remained long enough to provide a home for life. One of the onboard cameras can resolve objects as small as a dining table. The Mars Reconnaissance Orbiter (MRO) will also investigate potential landing sites and serve as a communications relay for future visits to the planet surface.

NEAR SHOEMAKER

NASA's Near Earth Asteroid Rendezvous (NEAR) Shoemaker spacecraft was launched in 1996 on a two-billion-mile (3.2-billion-km) journey to 433 Eros. NEAR Shoemaker rendezvoused with Eros in 2000 and imaged the asteroid from altitudes ranging from 200 miles (320km) to as low as 131 yards (120m). Its Multispectral Imaging System (MIS) mapped the asteroid's shape, landforms and colors. After one year of multiple orbits, NEAR Shoemaker was directed to make an unprecedented soft landing on the surface of Eros, where it continued to function for several weeks.

SPIRIT AND OPPORTUNITY

NASA's Mars Exploration Rovers (MERs), which landed on opposite sides of Mars in early 2004, are the first long-range robots to explore a planet's surface. These solar-powered, wheeled vehicles each have nine cameras. Three pairs of wide-angle stereo cameras on the front, rear and mast serve as navigational eyes for the probe. The fourth stereo pair is the color panoramic camera on the mast. This pair's narrow field of view and height approximate a human vantage point. A microscopic imager, located on the robotic arm of the Rover, can photograph extreme close-ups of rocks and soil.

STARDUST

Launched in 1999, NASA's Stardust is one of the few spacecraft to explore a comet. Its camera system has a Voyager wide-angle camera, a scan mirror to vary the viewing angle and a periscope to protect the mirror while the spacecraft flies through the comet coma. Stardust is the first robotic mission designed to return extraterrestrial material to Earth from beyond our moon. The probe collected dust and carbon-based samples during its closest encounter with comet Wild 2. Stardust's Sample Return Capsule made a parachute landing in the Utah desert in January 2006. Analysis of the samples indicates that comets could have delivered nitrogen-rich organic materials to jump-start life on the early Earth.

VIKING

NASA's Viking project sent two separate spacecraft to Mars in 1975. Each consisted of an orbiter and a lander. After orbiting Mars and returning images used for landing-site selection, the landers detached and soft-landed at the selected site. The orbiters continued imaging the planet — Viking 1 until 1979, Viking 2 until 1982. Each orbiter's Visual Imaging Subsystem consisted of twin high-resolution television cameras mounted on a scan platform.

VOYAGER 1 AND 2

Launched in 1977, NASA's Voyager 1 and 2 were the second set of probes to explore the outer solar system, following the Pioneer missions of the early 1970s. From 1979 to 1989, the twin Voyagers yielded

Viking

unprecedented images of Jupiter, Saturn, Uranus and Neptune, as well as their satellites and ring systems. The Voyagers each carried two cameras, a high-resolution narrow-angle and a lower-resolution wide-angle. The American astronomer Carl Sagan was responsible for creating the 12-inch (30-cm) gold-plated copper disc with images and sounds of Earth affixed to the outside of each probe. The Voyagers are traveling up to 90,000 miles (145,000km) per hour and are the most distant human-made objects in the universe.

INDIVIDUALS

Most images in COSMOS are by large institutional ground-based and space-based telescopes. But some of the most striking are by people working with accessible and mobile equipment.

FRED ESPENAK
is an astrophysicist at NASA's Goddard Space Flight Center in Greenbelt, Maryland, where he studies the atmospheres of planets. A recognized astrophotographer, he has published references on lunar and solar eclipses through 2035. Also known as "Mr. Eclipse," Espenak is the webmaster of NASA's official eclipse site.
<sunearth.gsfc.nasa.gov/eclipse>

BILL AND SALLY FLETCHER
typically work atop the White Mountains in California's Sierra Nevada. They make full-spectrum color imagery by shooting high-contrast and fine-grain black-and-white film in red, green and blue filtration. Their astrophotography has been published in NATIONAL GEOGRAPHIC, ASTRONOMY, SKY & TELESCOPE and Carl Sagan's PALE BLUE DOT.
<scienceandart.com>

STEFAN SEIP
is an information technology consultant in Stuttgart, Germany. He is also an astrophotographer who travels the world, but normally shoots from Germany's Black Forest region. Striving for authenticity, he believes that effective astrophotography is a love-match between art, physics, photography and chemical and digital processing.
<astromeeting.de>

AXEL MELLINGER
is a staff scientist in the Applied Condensed Matter Physics group at the University of Potsdam in Germany and a prominent astrophotographer who, over three years, took 51 photographs of the night sky from various locations around Earth. He then developed the software program that resulted in a seamless "all-sky" image of the Milky Way Galaxy in visible light. Mellinger used a Minolta SRT-101 and XD-5 camera with a 28mm lens riding piggyback on a Super Polaris DX mount.
<home.arcor-online.de/axel.mellinger/>

Mars Exploration Rover

GLOSSARY

asteroid
A rocky object smaller than a planet revolving around the Sun. Most asteroids are located between the orbits of Mars and Jupiter in an area known as the Asteroid Belt. They are primitive debris from the early solar system.

atmosphere
The layer of gases enveloping the surface or apparent surface of a star, planet or satellite.

aurora
Glowing gases seen above a planet's magnetic poles when charged particles in the solar wind collide with atoms in a planet's upper atmosphere. On Earth, they are known as aurora borealis or northern lights and aurora australis or southern lights. On Earth, the colors are produced by electrified oxygen and nitrogen atoms.

Barnard (B)
Prefix for numbering dark nebulas in Barnard's catalog, often abbreviated with a B. For example, the Horsehead Nebula can be designated as B 33.

Big Bang
The explosive event that is theorized to be the beginning of the universe.

binary star system
Two stars that are gravitationally bound together and orbit around their common center of mass.

black hole
An object in space that has almost no volume and infinite density. Its gravity is so strong that within a certain distance from it, nothing, not even light, can escape. A black hole is formed when a star more than ten times as massive as our Sun collapses and explodes in a supernova. A supermassive black hole with the mass of a million or more stars is thought to reside at the center of most galaxies.

blue supergiant
The most massive of the large, hot, bright stars. Their extremely high temperatures make them appear blue in color.

bulge, galactic
The spherical area composed of old stars, gas and dust at the center of spiral galaxies.

charged particles
Atomic particles with a negative (more electrons) or positive (more protons) electrical charge.

chromosphere
The layer of the Sun's atmosphere above the photosphere and below the corona. Composed mostly of hydrogen, it is roughly 6,200 miles (10,000km) thick. The chromosphere is hotter than the photosphere but not as hot as the corona.

comet
A body of rock and volatile ices that moves around the Sun in an eccentric orbit. Comets are small, typically only a few miles in diameter. When a comet is close to the Sun, the heat produces a coma of gas and dust that surrounds the nucleus of the comet. Solar radiation blows the gas and dust away, forming the comet's streaming tail.

constellation
A region of the sky outlined by a group of stars that form an imaginary figure as viewed from Earth. Constellations are named after mythological gods, heroes or animals. There are 88 constellations officially recognized by astronomers with precisely defined boundaries that cover the entire sky.

corona
The outermost gaseous layer of the solar atmosphere. The corona can be seen in visible light only when the central star area is blocked, as it is during a solar eclipse. The corona emits strongly in the extreme ultraviolet and X-ray wavelengths.

coronal loop
A huge arch of plasma that loops through the corona along a magnetic field line and connects a pair of sunspots of opposite magnetic polarity on the solar surface.

coronal mass ejection (CME)
A dramatic solar event in which plasma erupts from the solar surface into the Sun's upper atmosphere and travels rapidly through space.

cosmic microwave background
Electromagnetic radiation that fills space in every direction and at almost equal intensity. It is strongest in the microwave part of the spectrum and is commonly accepted to be the remnant afterglow of the Big Bang.

crater
A circular (or nearly circular) depression with a raised rim, usually caused by the impact of a comet or meteorite on the surface of a planet, satellite or asteroid. Some craters are caused by volcanic activity.

dark matter

Matter that cannot be observed because it does not emit electromagnetic radiation. Its existence is inferred by its gravitational influence in galaxy clusters and galactic halos as well as the warping of space measured by gravitational lensing.

dark nebula

An opaque cloud of gas and dust that appears as a silhouette in interstellar space. The nebula blocks out the visible light of the stars behind it.

disk, galactic

The flat disk of a galaxy composed of young stars, gas and dust in orbit around the center.

eclipse

A phenomenon in which one body passes in front of another so that the light from the background body is partially or totally obscured. In a solar eclipse, the Moon's shadow blocks the Sun's light from small portions of Earth's surface. In a lunar eclipse, the Moon passes through the shadow of Earth. Solar eclipses always occur near the time of the new Moon, lunar eclipses near the time of the full Moon.

electromagnetic radiation

A form of energy that travels through space as waves of electric and magnetic fields. Commonly called radiation or light, it spans the range from short wavelength gamma rays to long wavelength radio waves. The radiation our eyes can detect is known as visible light.

electromagnetic spectrum

The entire range of wavelengths for electromagnetic radiation, consisting of gamma rays, X-rays, ultraviolet, visible light, infrared, microwave and radio waves (in order from short to long wavelengths).

electron

An elementary particle with a negative charge and low mass. Electrons are bound to the nucleus of an atom by electromagnetic forces. An energized electron that breaks free of its atomic bond is known as a free electron.

elephant trunk

Along the walls of some nebulas long columns are created when hot ultraviolet light from nearby stars boils away the nebular gas. Within the nebula, dense globules of gas and dust resist the photoevaporation and shield the matter behind them. The globule and the protected material form a shape that resembles an elephant trunk.

emission nebula

A glowing cloud of interstellar gas laced with dust that emits light by being energized by the ultraviolet light of nearby stars.

event horizon

The outer boundary of a black hole. If matter travels across the border, the speed needed to escape the gravitational pull of the black hole would be greater than the speed of light.

flare

A sudden and violent explosion of solar energy, often observed near a sunspot and associated with coronal mass ejections.

galactic plane

The flattened area that defines the pancake-shaped disk of a galaxy. The plane contains the majority of the galaxy's stellar mass. Locations of celestial objects can be described as being above, below or in the plane.

Galilean satellites

Jupiter's four largest moons, discovered by Galileo through his telescope in 1610 – Io, Europa, Callisto and Ganymede.

globule

A dark, cold cloud of hydrogen that is often the predecessor of a star.

gravitational lens

A massive celestial object, such as a large galaxy or cluster of galaxies, that bends the light from objects behind it, magnifying the objects or causing multiple images of the same object.

gravity

The force of attraction between all matter in the universe. According to Isaac Newton's theory, gravitational attraction is stronger as the mass of two objects increases and as the distance between two objects decreases. Albert Einstein described gravity as the effect of space being warped by massive bodies.

greenhouse effect

Light entering a planet's atmosphere heats the surface and is converted into infrared radiation. The atmosphere of a planet contains certain gases, such as carbon dioxide, that do not allow this radiation to escape back into space, thus heating the planet's surface.

halo, galactic

The spherical region that envelops a spiral galaxy above and below the galactic disk. The halo contains globular clusters, dim stars, dark matter and a small amount of gas.

Hawking radiation

Radiation produced when virtual pairs of positive and negative charged particles are generated from the vacuum at the event horizon of a black hole. One particle escapes before being annihilated by its oppositely charged companion. This causes mass to leak away from the black hole, if it has no source for additional mass, until it eventually vanishes from existence.

Herbig-Haro (HH) object

A nebula produced by a protostar. The unusual nebula may be formed by gas jets streaming away from the star or by bombardment from the star's jets.

hydrogen-alpha (H-alpha)

Light emitted from an atomic transition in hydrogen appearing in the red portion of the visible-light spectrum. The wavelength is also emitted by plasma in the Sun's chromosphere.

IC

Prefix for numbers in the Index Catalog of non-stellar astronomical objects.

interstellar matter or medium

The gas and dust distributed between objects in a galaxy.

jets

Narrow, high-energy flow of matter from a central, gravitationally compact and energetic object. The jets typically stream in two opposite directions along the object's rotation axis.

Kuiper Belt

A region in the outer solar system inhabited by icy bodies that may be closely related to comets. It lies mostly in the ecliptic plane where the planets orbit the Sun. The belt extends from Neptune's orbit (2.8 billion miles/4.5 billion km from the Sun) to perhaps 30 times that distance. Pluto may be the largest known Kuiper Belt object.

light-year

The distance that light travels through a vacuum in one year — approximately six trillion miles (10 trillion km).

Local Group

The small cluster of galaxies in the neighborhood of the Milky Way. There are about 30 galaxies that are much smaller than the Milky Way. The spiral Andromeda Galaxy is the only other large galaxy in the Local Group.

M

A prefix for objects numbered in the Messier catalog of galaxies, star clusters and nebulas.

magnetic field

A force field around magnetized bodies, sometimes produced by electric currents flowing in loops. In the magnetic field surrounding the Sun and Earth, the north and south poles are linked by lines of magnetic force.

magnetic field lines

Imaginary lines that follow the intensity and movement of a magnetic field. Charged particles travel freely along magnetic field lines but are restricted from jumping lines by the force of the magnetic field.

nebula

Any diffuse cloud of interstellar gas and dust.

neutron star

A compact, extremely dense star formed from a stellar core that collapsed under gravity during a supernova. Composed almost entirely of neutrons, it has a radius of 3 to 12 miles (5 to 20km) and a mass of one to three times that of our Sun.

NGC

Prefix for numbers in the New General Catalog of non-stellar astronomical objects.

nuclear fusion

The process of combining two atomic nuclei to form a heavier nucleus. Energy is released in the process and fuels a star. The simplest form of fusion is the conversion of hydrogen to helium. Successive conversions build to increasingly heavier elements. This process requires the high temperatures and pressures typical of the deep interiors of stars.

nucleus, galactic

The central region of a galaxy, generally a few light-years in diameter. Most galactic nuclei host supermassive black holes.

Oort cloud

Large, spherical area surrounding our solar system where comets are thought to reside. The Oort cloud extends about 1.5 light-years from the Sun, about a third of the distance to our nearest stellar neighbor, Proxima Centauri.

ozone layer

The area in Earth's upper atmosphere with a strong concentration of ozone (molecules of oxygen with three atoms) that protects the planet from ultraviolet solar radiation.

photosphere

The visible surface of the Sun or a star.

planetary nebula
An envelope of glowing gas expelled by a star late in its life as it is transformed from a red giant to a white dwarf. Planetary nebulas come in a variety of shapes that offer forensic evidence about the star's late life behavior.

plasma
A fourth state of matter composed of superheated gases in the form of charged particles. Matter inside a star and most of the matter scattered across the universe is in the form of plasma.

prominence
A cloudlike structure in the Sun's atmosphere formed by an eruption of gas. Prominences have a lower temperature and higher density than their surroundings, causing them to be bright when viewed over the solar edge and dark against the solar disk.

proton
An elementary particle with a positive charge. The nuclei of atoms contain protons.

protostar
The first observable stage in star formation, before nuclear fusion begins.

pulsar
A rapidly spinning neutron star that emits powerful "lighthouse beacons" of electromagnetic radiation. This causes the star to appear to pulse at clocklike precision.

red giant
An old, large, cool star. A star expands to a red giant as the nuclear fusion process changes from fusing hydrogen atoms into helium atoms in the core to fusing hydrogen in a shell above the core.

reflection nebula
A cloud of gas and dust in interstellar space visible only by the light reflected from nearby stars.

retrograde
The atypical backward movement of certain planets and satellites.

shock wave
A wave caused by a sudden change in pressure. Examples are the shock waves created by a powerful explosion or the passing of a supersonic aircraft.

singularity
The center of a black hole where matter is compressed to infinite density and infinitesimal volume.

sol
A Martian day that is equivalent in Earth time to 24 hours, 39 minutes and 35 seconds.

solar cycle
The approximate 11-year period of solar activity caused by the entanglement and re-formation of the Sun's magnetic field. This cycle determines the frequency of sunspots, flares, loops and coronal mass ejections.

solar wind
Continuous flow of charged particles streaming away from the Sun into interplanetary space at millions of miles per hour.

speed of light
The speed at which electromagnetic radiation moves through empty space (about 186,000 miles/299,800km per second).

sunspot
A temporary patch on the photosphere of the Sun, which looks dark because it is cooler than its surroundings. The concentration of a strong magnetic field in the spot causes it to be cooler.

supergiant
A star with a radius between 100 and 1,000 times that of the Sun.

supernova
The explosive end of a massive star. The energetic output activates the expanding gases to radiate with a sharp increase in brilliance for weeks or months.

supernova remnant (SNR)
The glowing and expanding shell of gaseous material left over in a supernova explosion.

tectonic plates
Distinct mobile land masses that can make up the crust of a planet or satellite. Tectonic plates make up Earth's crust.

terrestrial planet
A planet composed mostly of rock. In our solar system, the four inner planets – Mercury, Venus, Earth and Mars – are terrestrial.

wavelength
The distance between successive crests or troughs of a wave.

white dwarf
The hot leftover core of a star the size of our Sun. In its final evolutionary stage, the star has used up its nuclear fuel and collapsed to a very small size.

INDEX

M

M 51 (galaxy), 252–3
M 82 (galaxy), 262–3
Magellan (spacecraft), 144–7, 305
Magellan, Ferdinand, 280
Magellan telecopes, 286, 300
Magellanic Clouds, 280–81
magnetic fields, 107, 110, 113, 114, 123, 310
Mare Orientale (Oriental Basin; Moon), 212–13
maria, lunar, 212–13
Mariner 10, 143, 158, 305
Mars, 158–75
   atmosphere/climate of, 161–2
   canals on, 158
   color of, 166, 296, 298
   fascination with, 158–9
   life on, 158–61
   moons of, 166, 209, 216–17
   naming of, 158
   size of, 158
   surface of, 162–6
   temperatures on, 162
   water on, 158–9
Mars Exploration Rovers (MERs), 159, 160–61, 166, 306, 307
Mars Express (spacecraft), 162, 168–72, 304, 305
Mars Global Surveyor (MGS), 159, 164, 305
Mars Odyssey (spacecraft), 172, 305–6
Mars Reconnaissance Orbiter (spacecraft), 162, 166, 305–6
Mellinger, Axel, 307
Mercury, 142–3
   naming of, 143
   orbit/rotation of, 143
   surface of, 143
   temperatures on, 143
   transits of, 149
   water on, 143
Meridiani Planum (Mars), 161
Merope, 58–9

MERs (Mars Exploration Rovers), 159, 160–61, 166, 306, 307
Messier catalog, 310
meteoroids, 176, 182
methane, 160–61
Metis (moon of Jupiter), 182
MGS (Mars Global Surveyor), 159, 164, 305
The Mice (NGC 4676 A and B; galaxies), 272–3
Milky Way, 10–11, 246–7
   as a barred spiral galaxy, 255
   center of, 269
   dwarf galaxies in, 248
   globular clusters in, 74
   hydrogen in, 290–91
   in the Local Group, 246
   and the Magellanic Clouds, 258
   galactic plane of, 270–71
   red dwarfs in, 68
   size of, 250
   solar system's location in, 10–11
Mimas (moon of Saturn), 188–9, 191, 230–31
Miner, Ellis D., 196
Mini-Spiral (Milky Way), 269
Miranda (moon of Uranus), 196
molecular clouds, 22–5
Monocerotis, 88–91
Moon, 210–15
   astronauts on, 212, 214–15
   axis/rotation of, 211
   formation of, 212
   gravity on, 212
   myth/mystery surrounding, 211
   "the new Moon in the old Moon's arms," 320
   Oriental Basin, 212–13
   phases of, 211
   solar eclipses caused by, 131
   surface of, 212
moons. See satellites
Mount Etna (Earth), 154
M prefix, 310
MSX Satellite, 292–3, 302

N

National Optical Astronomy Observatory (NOAO), 4, 22, 30, 33, 36, 38, 41, 52, 55, 202, 258, 278, 300
National Radio Astronomy Observatory (NRAO), 93, 278, 291, 301
Near Earth Asteroid Rendezvous (NEAR) Shoemaker, 176, 306
nebulas, 12–65
   Barnard's Merope Nebula, 62–3
   Boomerang Nebula, 62
   Bubble Nebula, 38–9
   Bug Nebula, 48–9
   Cat's Eye Nebula, 49, 50–51
   Cone Nebula, 42–3
   Crab Nebula, 92–5
   dark, 15, 42
   defined, 310
   Dumbbell Nebula, 52
   Eagle Nebula, 24–5
   Egg Nebula, 45, 46–7
   Elephant's Trunk Nebula, 28–9
   emission, 15, 28–30
   Firestorm Nebula, 68–9
   Flame Nebula, 17
   Flaming Star Nebula, 33
   globules in, 15, 26–31, 68
   Helix Nebula, 100–101
   Horsehead Nebula, 16–17, 20–21, 26
   Orion Nebula Complex, 16–21
   Pelican Nebula, 41
   planetary, 15, 45–9, 52, 71, 311
   Red Rectangle Nebula, 52–3
   reflection, 15, 42, 58–9
   Ring Nebula, 44–5
   Rosette Nebula, 4
   Snake Nebula, 24
   stars' death in, 15
   supernova remnants (SNRs), 15, 54–5, 311

Tarantula Nebula, 40–41
Veil Nebula, 55, 56–7
Witch Head Nebula, 60–61
Neptune, 198–9
   atmosphere/winds of, 199
   color of, 199, 296
   discovery of, 199
   gaseous composition of, 199
   moons of, 199, 242–3
   naming of, 199
   orbit of, 199
   rings of, 199
   size/mass of, 199
neutral hydrogen, 291
neutron stars, 71, 82, 86, 310
New Horizons mission, 200
NGC, 310
NGC 1316 (galaxy), 256–7
NGC 2207 (galaxy), 274–5
NGC 2787 (galaxy), 266
NGC 3079 (galaxy), 260–61
NGC 3370 (galaxy), 250–51
NGC 4622 (galaxy), 266
NGC 4676 A and B ("The Mice"; galaxies), 272–3
NGC 6822 (galaxy), 258–9
NGC 7424 (galaxy), 254–5
NOAO (National Optical Astronomy Observatory), 4, 22, 30, 33, 36, 38, 41, 52, 55, 202, 258, 278, 300
Northern Hemisphere (Earth), 151
novas, 84–8
NRAO (National Radio Astronomy Observatory), 93, 278, 291, 301
nuclear fusion, 68, 73, 106, 147–8, 179, 310
nucleus, galactic, 310

O

Oberon (moon of Uranus), 196
observatories/telescopes, 300–304
Olduvai Gorge (Tanzania), 155
Olympus Mons (Mars), 166
Omega Centauri, 76
Oort Cloud, 203, 310

PICTURE CREDITS

Image optimization:
Will Hopkins, Hopkins/Baumann, and Michael Soluri, Michael Soluri Photography

Anglo-Australian Observatory:
© Anglo-Australian & Royal Edinburgh Observatory/David Malin Images, 16–17

Apollo 12 / Apollo 17:
NASA/JSC, 133, 211, 214–15

Canada-France-Hawaii Telescope:
© Canada-France-Hawaii-Telescope–J. C. Cuillandre/Coelum, 20–21, 28, 42, 300

Cassini Orbiter: NASA/JPL/SCI, 136, 178–9, 184–95, 208, 222–3, 230–34, 238–41; NASA/JPL/USGS, 237

Chandra X-Ray Observatory:
NASA/CXC/SAO, 92 (with Hubble), 93 (X-ray), 96, 269, 301; NASA/JPL-Caltech/STSci/CXC/UofA/ESA/AURA/JHU, 262; NASA/CXC/STSci/ESO WFI/Magellan/U.Arizona, 287

Clementine: SDIO/NASA, 320

Compton Gamma Ray Observatory: NASA, 296 (gamma)

Cosmic Background Explorer: NASA, 298 (infrared)

Deep Impact Mission: NASA/JPL/UMD, 205

Fred Espenak: © Fred Espenak, 130

European Southern Observatory: © European Southern Observatory, 40, 59, 76, 196, 254; NASA/CXC/STSci/ESO WFI/Magellan/U.Arizona, 287

Bill and Sally Fletcher: © Bill and Sally Fletcher/Science and Art, 19

GALEX (Galaxy Evolution Explorer): NASA/GALEX/Caltech/JPL, 1, 278 (with Spitzer)

Galileo: NASA/JPL-Caltech, 182 (with Voyager 2), 183, 210, 218, 224–8

Gemini Observatory:
© Association of Universities for Research in Astronomy, Inc., 8–9, 276–7

Hubble Space Telescope:
NASA/ESA, 6–7, 18, 24, 27, 43, 46–7, 48–51, 53, 62–3, 68–9, 77–81, 84–91, 92 (with Chandra), 94–5, 98, 101, 121, 137–8, 140–41, 197, 201, 246–53, 257, 260–61, 264–7, 272–5, 284–5, 288–9 (with Max-Planck); NASA/JPL-Caltech/STSci/CXC/UofA/ESA/AURA/JHU, 262; NASA/CXC/STSci/ESO WFI/Magellan/ U.Arizona, 287

Huygens Probe: ESA/NASA/JPL/University of Arizona, 235–6

International Ultraviolet Explorer: NASA, 297 (ultraviolet)

Johns Hopkins University/Applied Physics Laboratory (JHUAPL): NASA/Goddard Space Flight Center, University of Iowa, Johns Hopkins University/Applied Physics Laboratory, 118 (with Polar and Terra)

Landsat:
NASA/GSFC, 152–3 (with Shuttle Radar Topography Mission)

Lunar Orbiter 4:
NASA/GSFC, 212–13, 305

Magellan Spacecraft:
NASA/JPL-Caltech, 144–7

Magellan Telescope:
NASA/CXC/STSci/ESO WFI/Magellan/U.Arizona, 287

Mariner 10:
NASA/JPL-Caltech, 142–3

Mars Exploration Rovers: NASA/JPL-Caltech, 160–61; NASA/JPL/Cornell, 166 (center), 307 (bottom)

Mars Express:
ESA/DLR/FU Berlin (G. Neukum), 163, 168–71, 174–5, 304

Mars Global Surveyor:
NASA/JPL/MSSS, 158–9, 164–5

Mars Reconnaissance Orbiter:
NASA/JPL-Caltech/University of Arizona, 162, 166 (bottom), 167

Max-Planck-Institute for Astronomy: GEMS © Max-Planck-Institute for Astronomy, 288–9 (with Hubble)

Axel Mellinger:
© Axel Mellinger, 298 (visible light)

MSX Satellite: AFRL/BMDO, 292–3

NEAR Shoemaker:
NASA/JHUAPL, 176–7

NOAO (National Optical Astronomy Observatory): NRAO/AUI/NOAO/AURA/NSF, 2, 259, 279; NOAO/AURA/NSF, 4–5, 23, 30–33, 38–9, NOAO, 37 (right); University of Colorado, University of Hawaii and NOAO/AURA/NSF, 41; WIYN/NSF, 52; NOAO/AURA/NSF/© WIYN Consortium, Inc., All Rights Reserved, 56–7, 202 (left)

NRAO: © National Radio Astronomy Observatory (NRAO/AUI/NSF), 93 (radio), 290–91, 299 (radio)

Palomar Observatory: ESA, AURA, Caltech, 74–5; Davide De Martin <skyfactory.org>/Acknowledgment: Digitized Sky Survey, 83; courtesy Paul Scowen/Jeff Hester (Arizona State University), 93 (visible)

Polar: NASA/GSFC/NOAA, 118 (with JHUAPL and Terra)

Roentgen Satellite:
NASA/GSFC, 297 (X-rays)

Stefan Seip:
© Stefan Seip, 148–9

Shuttle Radar Topography Mission:
NASA/JPL/NGA, 152–3 (with Landsat), 155

SOHO (Solar and Heliospheric Observatory): SOHO (ESA & NASA), 105–7, 108, 116–17, 127–9, 302

Spitzer Space Telescope: NASA/JPL-Caltech, 14, 29, 34–5, 36 (left 3), 44, 54, 60–61, 64–5, 70–73, 139, 202–3 (main), 270–71, 278 (with GALEX), 281; NASA/JPL-Caltech/STSci/CXC/UofA/ESA/AURA/JHU, 262

Stardust: NASA/JPL-Caltech, 204, 306

Swedish 1m Solar Telescope:
© Royal Swedish Academy of Sciences/Lockheed Martin Solar & Astrophysics Laboratory, 109; © Royal Swedish Academy of Sciences, 122, 124–5

Terra: NASA/GSFC, 118 (with JHUAPL and Polar), 150–51; NASA/JPL-Caltech, 154, 156–7

TRACE: NASA/Lockheed Martin Solar Advanced Laboratory, 112, 115

2MASS:
2MASS/UMass/IPAC-Caltech/NASA/NSF, 10–11, 93 (infrared), 268

2001 Mars Odyssey: NASA/JPL/Arizona State University, 172–3

Viking:
NASA/JPL/GSFC, 217, 307 (top)

Voyager: NASA/JPL-Caltech, 181, 182 (with Galileo), 198–9, 220–21, 229, 242–3

WMAP (Wilkinson Microwave Anisotropy Probe): NASA/WMAP Science Team, 294–5, 299 (microwaves), 303

Yohkoh:
ISAS–Japan/NASA/LMSAL, 111

ACKNOWLEDGMENTS

This book could not have been completed without the invaluable assistance of the scientists and space professionals who generously shared their knowledge and helped us understand the nature of the universe.

George Coyne, SJ/Director, Vatican Observatory
Christopher Corbally, SJ/Vice-Director, Vatican Observatory Research Group
Tom Pelly, Graduate Assistant to Professor Stephen Hawking, Department of Applied Mathematics and Theoretical Physics, University of Cambridge
Orlando Figueroa, Deputy Associate Administrator for Programs, Science Mission Directorate, NASA
Ellis D. Miner, Ph.D., JPL Science Division/Co-director NASA Solar System Exploration Education and Public Outreach Forum
Nicola J. Fox, Ph.D., Living with a Star/Geospace Project Scientist, Johns Hopkins University/Applied Physics Laboratory
Jet Propulsion Laboratory/ California Institute of Technology: Franklin O'Donnell, Publications, Office Manager; Carolina Martinez, Guy Webster, Alice Wessen, Alan Buis, Whitney Clavin, Jane Platt, Charli Schuler, with additional support from Phil Christensen, Noel Gorelick, Ken Edgett and Brian Cooper
Mars Space Flight Facility, Arizona State University: Philip R. Christensen, Ph.D, Robert Burnham, Chris Edwards

European Southern Observatory: Education and Public Relations Department: Elisabeth Voelk, Secretary; Henri Boffin, Ph.D., Editor; Ed Janssen, Graphics; Hans-Hermann Heyer, Photographer/ Exhibitions
Zoe Frank and **Karel Schrijver**, Ph.D., Lockheed Martin Solar & Astrophysics Lab
Steele Hill, Ph.D., SOHO Media Specialist, NASA/Goddard Space Flight Center
Charles L. Bennett, Ph.D., Principal Investigator WMAP, NASA/Goddard Space Flight Center
Felix J. Lockman, Ph.D., Scientist, National Radio Astronomy Observatory, Green Bank
Stephan D. Price, Ph.D., Division Scientist, VSB/Space Vehicles Directorate Air Force Research Laboratory
Michael Skrutskie, Ph.D., Principal Investigator, 2MASS
Jean-Charles Cuillandre, Ph.D., Astronomer, Canada-France-Hawaii Telescope Corporation
Travis A. Rector, Ph.D., University of Alaska, Anchorage
Bo Reipurth, Ph.D., Institute for Astronomy, University of Hawaii
Kathie Coil, Program Coordinator, NOAO Office of Public Affairs & Educational Outreach
Kevin Luhman, Ph.D., Harvard-Smithsonian Center for Astrophysics

Brian R. Dennis, Ph.D, Astrophysicist, Solar Physics Branch, Laboratory for Astronomy and Solar Physics, NASA/Goddard Space Flight Center
David Watkins, Ph.D., Program Manager, Laboratory-Directed Research & Development, Los Alamos National Laboratory
Prof Dr Gerhard Neukum, Institute of Geosciences, Freie Universitaet, Berlin, and his Team at FU-Berlin
Jan-Peter Muller, Ph.D., Department of Geomatic Engineering, University College London
John Murray, Ph.D., Department of Earth Sciences, The Open University, Milton Keynes
Martin G. Tomasko, Ph.D., Lunar and Planetary Laboratory, University of Arizona
Michael J. Mumma, Ph.D., Chief Scientist, Planetary Research Laboratory for Extraterrestrial Physics, and Director, The Goddard Center for Astrobiology, NASA/GSFC
Paul D. Spudis, Planetary Scientist, Johns Hopkins University/Applied Physics Laboratory
W. Butler Burton, Ph.D., Leiden University Observatory, National Radio Astronomy Observatory
Boris Häußler, Ph.D. student, GEMS, Max-Planck-Institute for Astronomy
Alan Bean, artist and the fourth human to walk on the Moon (Apollo 12)
Mats Löfdahl, Ph.D., and **Dan Kiselman**, Ph.D., Institute for Solar Physics, The Royal Swedish Academy of Sciences

NASA/Johnson Space Center: Eileen M. Hawley, Director/Public Affairs; David Youngman and Steve Nesbitt, Public Affairs Office; Michael Gentry and Susan D. Erskin, Media Resource Center; Mary Wilkerson, Still Imagery Repository Supervisor; Juan R. Zamora, Imaging Science; Edward B. Wilson, Television and Photographic Operations; Cayce Cox, Rodney Dowell, Warren Harold, Rob Ingram, Photographic Operations Group

National Space Science Data Center: Jay S. Friedlander, Visualization Lab; Leon Kosofsky/Lunar Orbiter; Dave Williams, Ph.D., Planetary Acquisition Scientist; Michael H. Carr, Ph.D./Viking Orbiter, NASA/Goddard Space Flight Center

D. Christopher Martin, Ph.D., Principal Investigator, Galaxy Evolution Explorer (GALEX), California Institute of Technology

George Jacoby, Ph.D., Director, WIYN Observatory

Bart De Pontieu, Ph.D., Lockheed Martin Solar & Astrophysics Lab

Robert L. Hurt, Ph.D., Imaging Scientist, Spitzer Science Center

Peter Edmonds, Ph.D., Chandra Press Scientist, Chandra X-Ray Observatory/Harvard University

Robert E. Crippen, Ph.D., Research Geologist, NASA/JPL

Denis Bogan, Ph.D., Program Scientist: Cassini/Huygens Mission to Saturn and Titan, New Horizons Mission to Pluto/Charon and the Kuiper Belt, NASA

Joseph L. Hora, Ph.D., Harvard-Smithsonian Center for Astrophysics

Edward B. Churchwell, Ph.D., Department of Astronomy, University of Wisconsin-Madison

Douglas Clowe, Ph.D., Department of Physics and Astronomy, Ohio University

Joseph L. Hora, Ph.D., Harvard-Smithsonian Center for Astrophysics

Peter Michaud, Public Information and Outreach Manager, The Gemini Observatory

Nadia Imbert-Vier, European Space Agency, Production Iconographique et Multimédia, Division de la Communication

David Herring, Earth Sciences Directorate, Education and Public Outreach, Committee Coordinator, NASA/Goddard Space Flight Center

Loren W. Acton, Ph.D., Department of Physics, University of Montana

James Irons, Ph.D., Biospheric Sciences, NASA/Goddard Space Flight Center

Nathan Smith, Ph.D., University of California, Berkeley Astronomy Department

Robert Simmon, Earth Sciences Directorate, Visualizer, NASA/Goddard Space Flight Center

Robin J. Barnes, Space Department, Johns Hopkins University/Applied Physics Laboratory

John Bally, Ph.D., University of Colorado at Boulder, Center for Astrophysics and Space Astronomy

Rachel Somerville, Ph.D., Astronomer, Archive Scientist, Space Telescope Science Institute

Mary Ann Hager, Data Manager, Lunar and Planetary Institute

Margaret Persinger, Kennedy Space Center

Helen Worth and **Kristi Marren**, Office of Public Affairs, Johns Hopkins University/Applied Physics Laboratory

Charles Blue, Public Information Officer, National Science Foundation

Lee Shapiro, Ph.D., Head, Education and Public Outreach, National Radio Astronomy Observatory

Lynda Seaver, Lawrence Livermore National Laboratory

Lynn Chandler, Public Affairs Officer, Earth Observing System, NASA/Goddard Space Flight Center

Leslie Bell, Media Relations, University College London Development and Corporate Communications Office

Louis De La Forêt, Media Relations Officer, The Open University, Milton Keynes

Barbara Poppe and **Daniel C. Wilkinson**, Space Environment Center, National Oceanic and Atmospheric Administration

Adrienne Wasserman, Astrogeology Team, U.S. Geological Survey

A heartfelt thanks to those near and dear to us for their patience, understanding and support.

Caroline Herter and Debbie Berne
Emerson Bruns, Esq.

FOR SOLURI & NOLLETTI:
Andre, Patrick and Gabriel Soluri
Joseph F. and Jane E. Soluri
Albert A. Nolletti
David Stefanou
Gene Lynch
Kevin Fuscus
Maria-Judite dos Santos
Lisa Freudenberger
East 87th Street Tribe
Charles Arnold, Jr.
Roger Remington
Ernst Both
Frank Able

FOR HOPKINS/BAUMANN:
Jerry and Kay Baumann
Sarah Hopkins
David and Polly Hopkins
Tom and Leslie Baumann
Turner and Carlene Hopkins
Martha Hopkins
Nick and Michael Baumann
Nick and Maddy Hopkins
Ira Mothner and Linda Fennimore
Son Do and Erica Aitken
Mary Beth Brewer
Stella Sands
Gaby and Bill Scully
Anthony Blake and Kyle Hayes
Charlie Dixon
John Stark
Steven Erickson and Michele Oppliger
R. Smith Schuneman
Lois Dolphin, BVM
Valerie Kriesel
Sr. Jeannine Percy, OSM

EARTHSHINE

Light and the absence of light make up the language of the skies. As we learn better how to read the heavens, we discover more of what's out there. Starlight speaks to us from long ago as well as far away, and stretches of deep darkness, where nothing glows, sometimes reveal as much as brilliant supernovas.

Shown here are the brightest objects in our sky. The Moon, in the foreground, partially masks a rising Sun, while the planet Venus glows pink beyond them. But while the objects are familiar, the view is not, for the radiant three have been photographed not from Earth, but from the spacecraft Clementine.

Where then is Earth? The clue is that bright stretch of moonscape on the right. Since what illuminates this sector of the Moon cannot be the Sun, it must be what we call "earthshine" – sunlight that is reflected off Earth (or, more precisely, off the clouds in Earth's atmosphere). That means Earth is somewhere off to the right, just out of the picture.

We see earthshine from Earth when the Sun illuminates a crescent Moon. Beside the shining crescent, the rest of the Moon is barely visible in the dim glow of earthshine. The phenomenon has been called "the new Moon in the old Moon's arms."

Earthshine is of growing interest to astronomers. It is a tantalizing piece of celestial language they seek to find repeated elsewhere in the universe – a telltale trace of other Earth-like planets out beyond our solar system.

**SUNRISE AND VENUS
OVER THE MOON**

EARTHSHINE ILLUMINATES
THE RIGHT SIDE OF THE MOON

VISIBLE-LIGHT IMAGE
(COLOR ADDED)

CLEMENTINE SPACECRAFT

1,465 MILES (2,358KM)
FROM CLEMENTINE

5 MARCH 1994

238,868 MILES (384,403KM)
FROM EARTH TO MOON